ROBIN HOOD
OUTLAW OF SHERWOOD FOREST

AN
ENGLISH
LEGEND

GRAPHIC UNIVERSE™

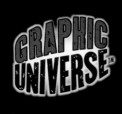

STORY BY
PAUL D. STORRIE

PENCILS AND INKS BY
THOMAS YEATES

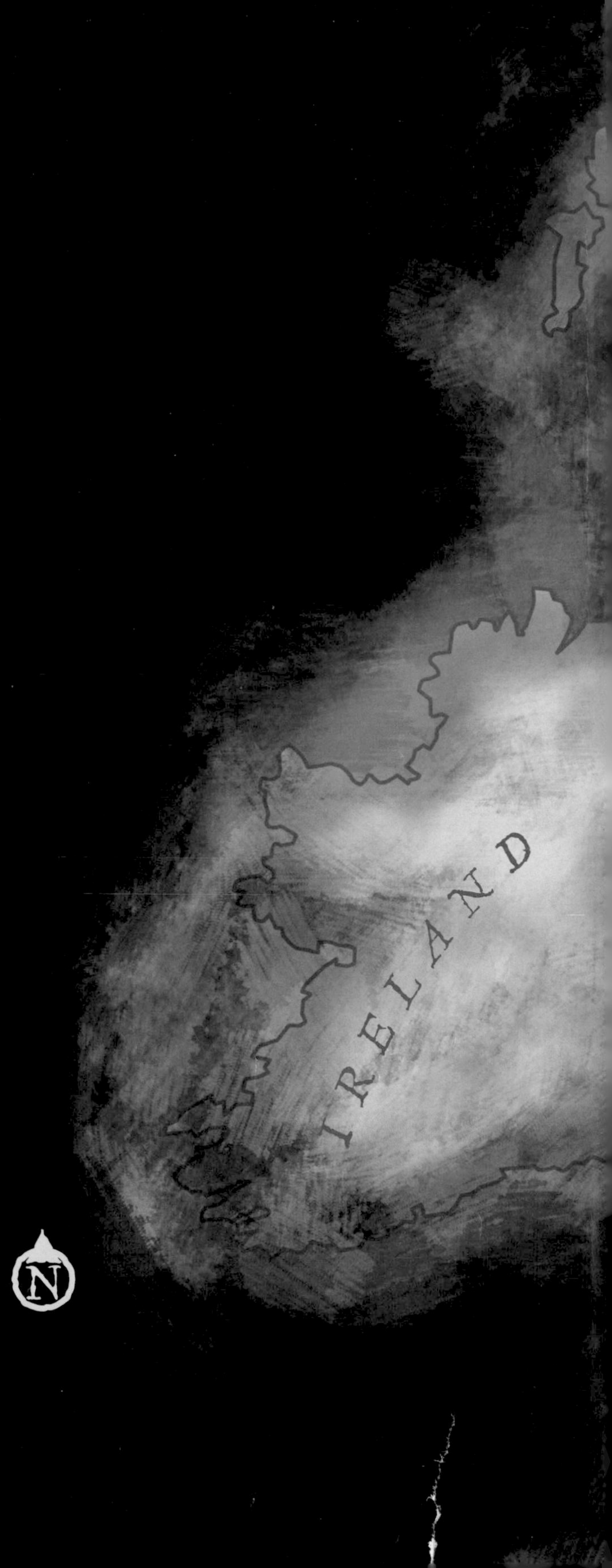
IRELAND
N

ROBIN HOOD

OUTLAW OF SHERWOOD FOREST

AN ENGLISH LEGEND

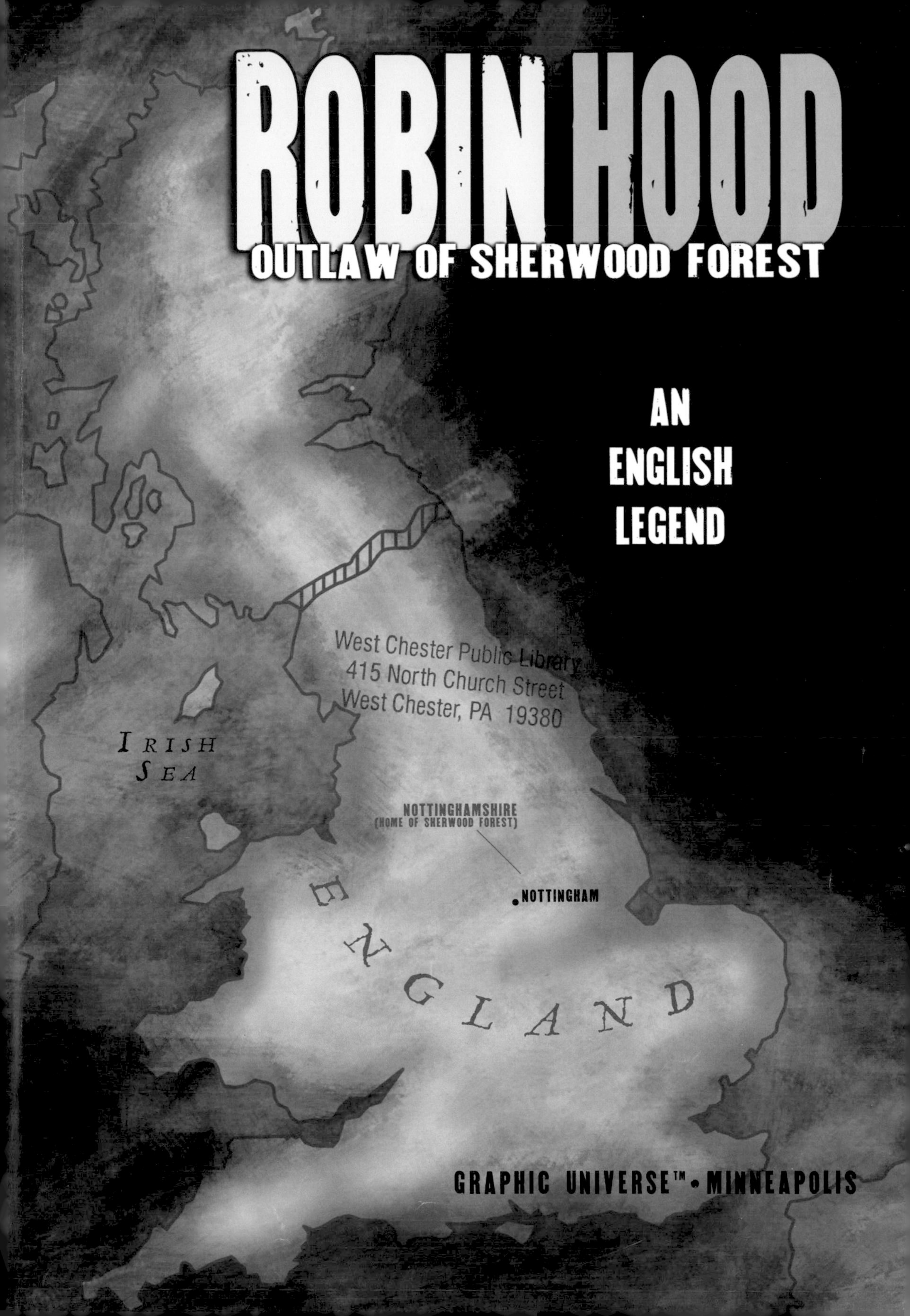
IRISH SEA
NOTTINGHAMSHIRE (HOME OF SHERWOOD FOREST)
NOTTINGHAM
ENGLAND

GRAPHIC UNIVERSE™ • MINNEAPOLIS

Robin Hood may or may not have been an actual person. Real or not, his adventures have delighted readers, listeners, and viewers for centuries. To write this particular book, author Paul D. Storrie relied heavily on the earliest versions of the Robin Hood stories available: the lyrics to the medieval songs about Robin and his followers. His research also included the excellent books *Robin Hood* by J. C. Holt and *Robin Hood: A Complete Study of the English Outlaw* by Stephen Thomas Knight. Artist Thomas Yeates referred to books by great illustrators of the past, including Howard Pyle, Harold Foster, and N. C. Wyeth.

STORY BY PAUL D. STORRIE

PENCILS AND INKS BY THOMAS YEATES

COLORING BY HI-FI DESIGN

LETTERING BY BILL HAUSER

CONSULTANT: ANDREW SCHEIL
ASSISTANT PROFESSOR OF ENGLISH,
UNIVERSITY OF MINNESOTA

Copyright © 2007 by Millbrook Press, Inc.

Graphic Universe™ is a trademark of Millbrook Press, Inc.

Graphic Universe™
An imprint of Lerner Publishing Group
241 First Avenue North
Minneapolis, MN 55401 U.S.A.

Website address: www.lernerbooks.com

Library of Congress Cataloging-in-Publication Data

Storrie, Paul D.
    Robin Hood : outlaw of Sherwood Forest / by Paul D. Storrie ; illustrations by Thomas Yeates.
        p.   cm. — (Graphic myths and legends)
    Summary: Recounts the life and adventures of Robin Hood, who, with his band of followers, lived in Sherwood Forest as an outlaw dedicated to fighting tyranny. Presented in comic book format.
        ISBN-13: 978-0-8225-5964-1 (lib. bdg. : alk. paper)
        ISBN-10: 0-8225-5964-1 (lib. bdg. : alk. paper)
        1. Robin Hood (Legendary character)—Legends.
    [1. Robin Hood (Legendary character)—Legends.
    2. Folklore—England. 3. Cartoons and comics.]
    I. Yeates, Thomas, ill. II. Robin Hood (Legend)
    III. Title. IV. Series.
    PZ8.1.S8845Ro 2007
    [398.2]—dc22   2006003707

Manufactured in the United States of America
1 2 3 4 5 6 - JR - 12 11 10 09 08 07

TABLE OF CONTENTS

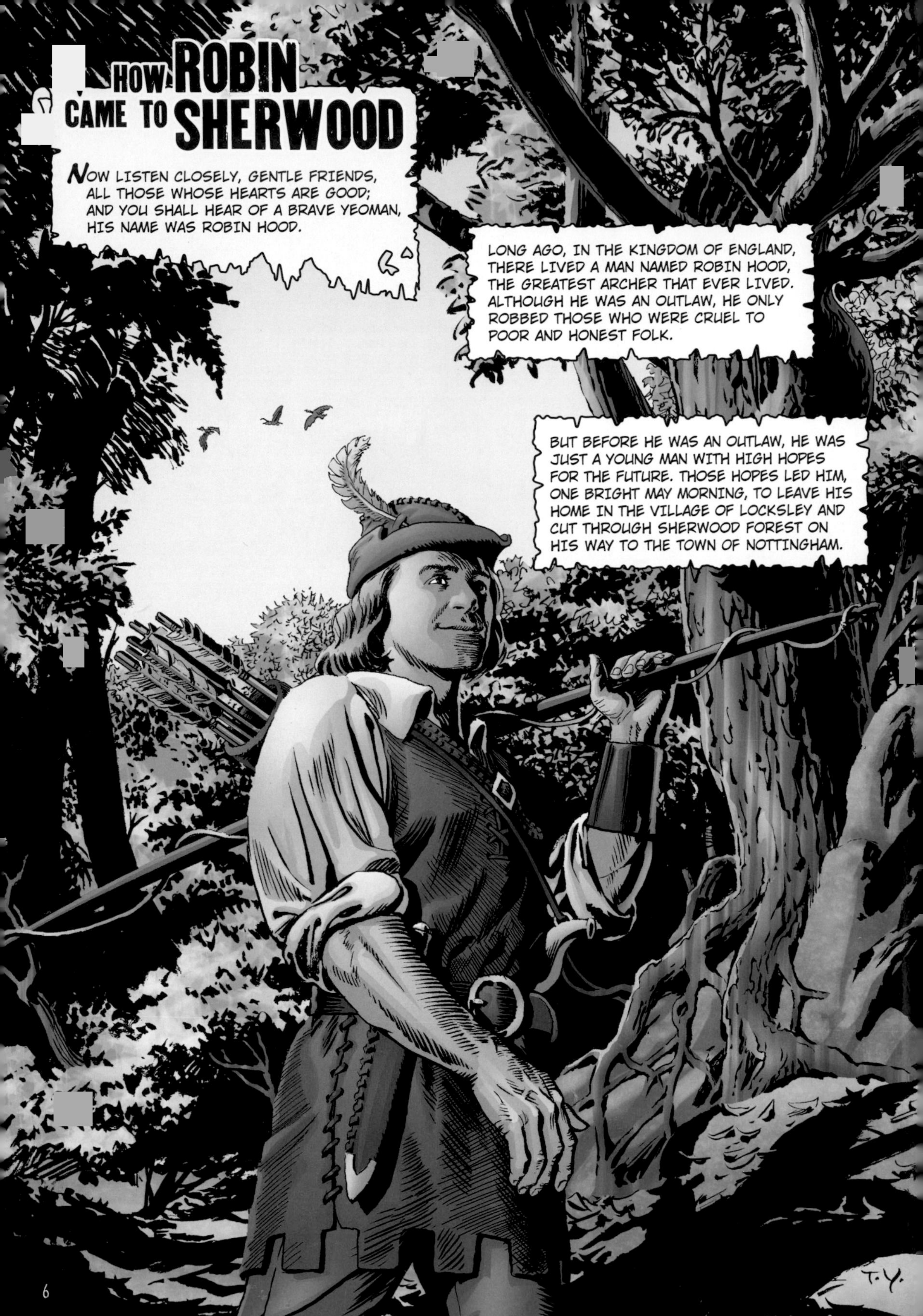
HOW ROBIN CAME TO SHERWOOD
NOW LISTEN CLOSELY, GENTLE FRIENDS, ALL THOSE WHOSE HEARTS ARE GOOD; AND YOU SHALL HEAR OF A BRAVE YEOMAN, HIS NAME WAS ROBIN HOOD.
LONG AGO, IN THE KINGDOM OF ENGLAND, THERE LIVED A MAN NAMED ROBIN HOOD, THE GREATEST ARCHER THAT EVER LIVED. ALTHOUGH HE WAS AN OUTLAW, HE ONLY ROBBED THOSE WHO WERE CRUEL TO POOR AND HONEST FOLK.
BUT BEFORE HE WAS AN OUTLAW, HE WAS JUST A YOUNG MAN WITH HIGH HOPES FOR THE FUTURE. THOSE HOPES LED HIM, ONE BRIGHT MAY MORNING, TO LEAVE HIS HOME IN THE VILLAGE OF LOCKSLEY AND CUT THROUGH SHERWOOD FOREST ON HIS WAY TO THE TOWN OF NOTTINGHAM.
T.Y.

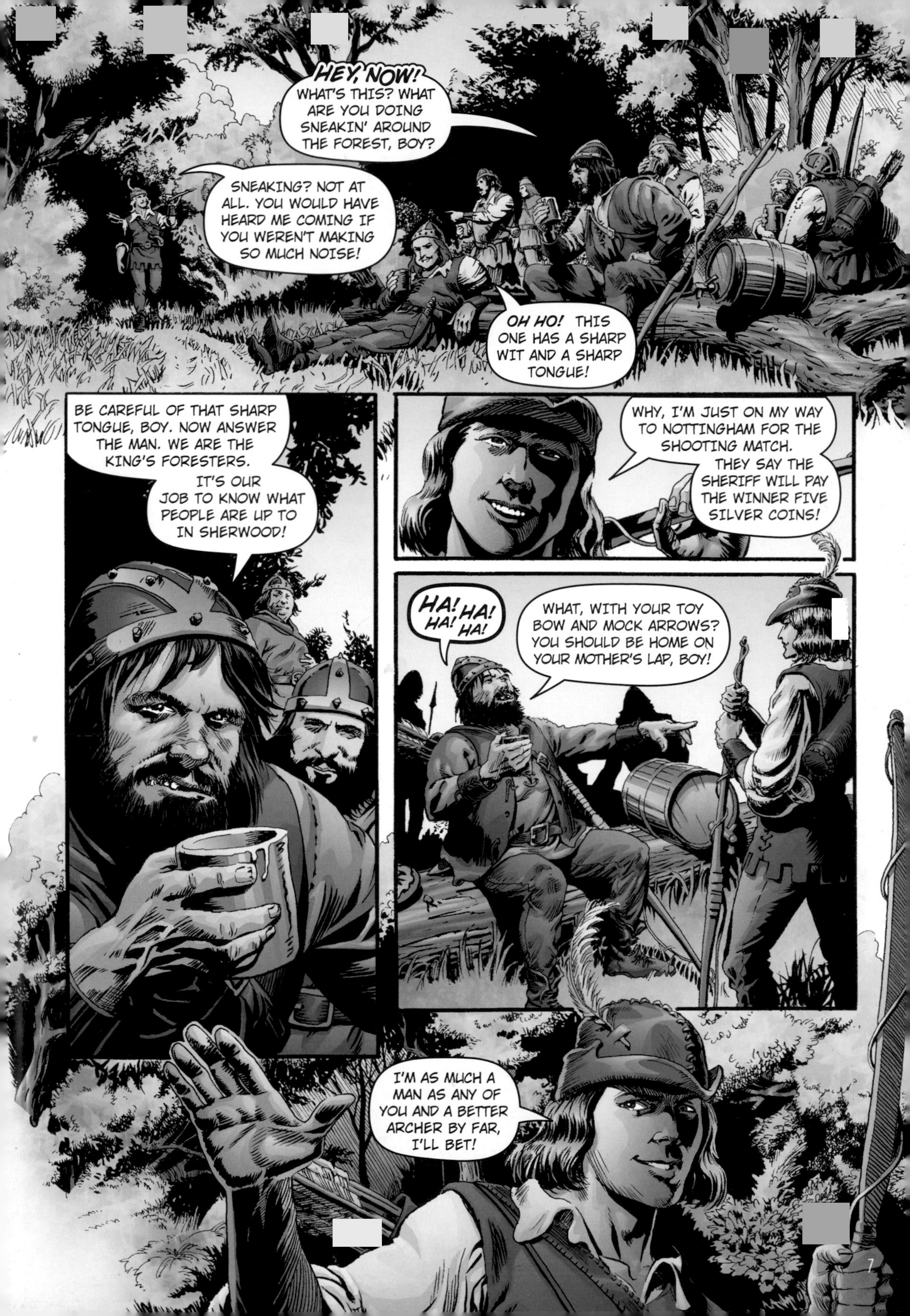
HEY, NOW! WHAT'S THIS? WHAT ARE YOU DOING SNEAKIN' AROUND THE FOREST, BOY?
SNEAKING? NOT AT ALL. YOU WOULD HAVE HEARD ME COMING IF YOU WEREN'T MAKING SO MUCH NOISE!
OH HO! THIS ONE HAS A SHARP WIT AND A SHARP TONGUE!
BE CAREFUL OF THAT SHARP TONGUE, BOY. NOW ANSWER THE MAN. WE ARE THE KING'S FORESTERS.
IT'S OUR JOB TO KNOW WHAT PEOPLE ARE UP TO IN SHERWOOD!
WHY, I'M JUST ON MY WAY TO NOTTINGHAM FOR THE SHOOTING MATCH.
THEY SAY THE SHERIFF WILL PAY THE WINNER FIVE SILVER COINS!
HA! HA! HA! HA!
WHAT, WITH YOUR TOY BOW AND MOCK ARROWS? YOU SHOULD BE HOME ON YOUR MOTHER'S LAP, BOY!
I'M AS MUCH A MAN AS ANY OF YOU AND A BETTER ARCHER BY FAR, I'LL BET!

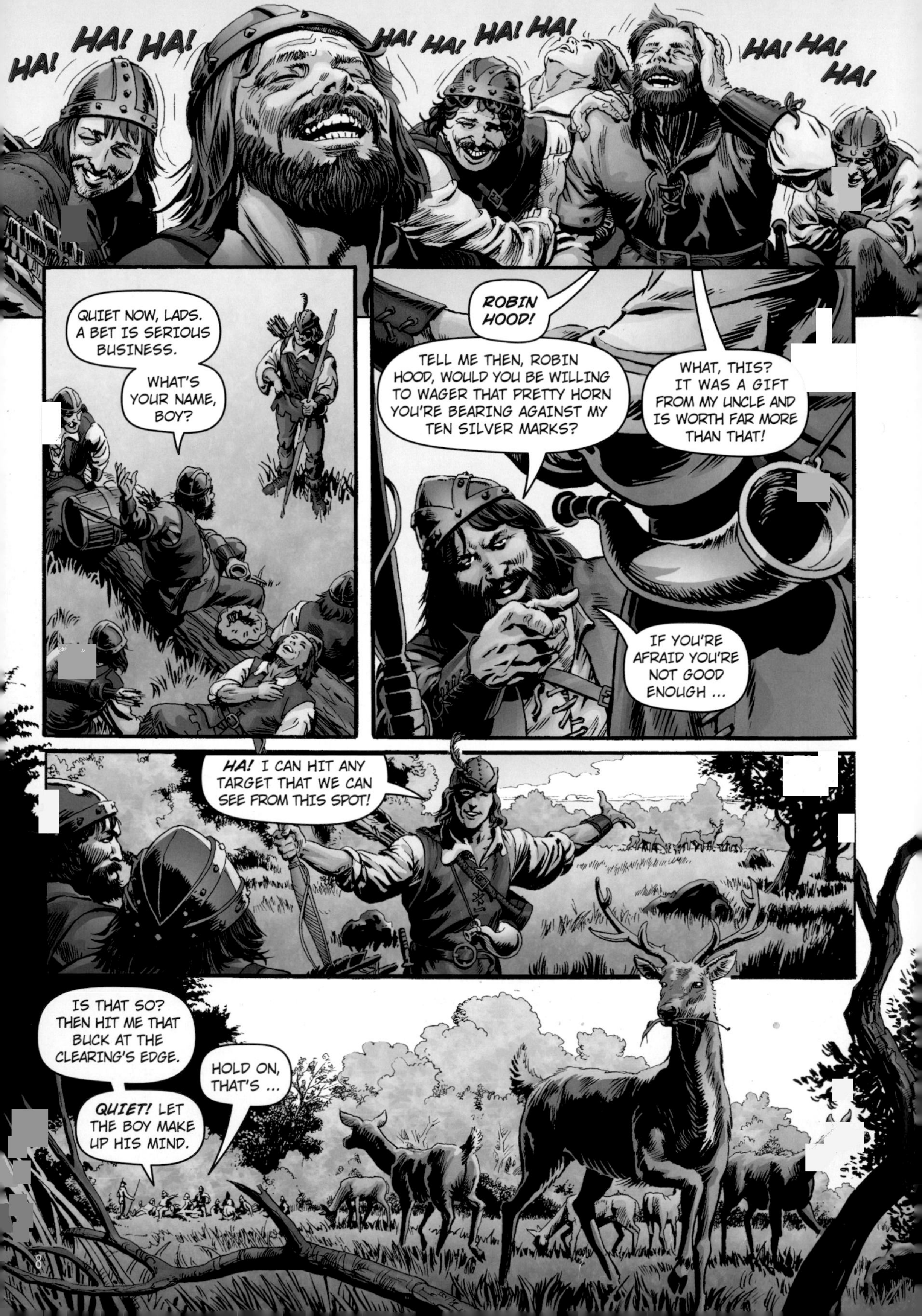
HA! HA! HA!
HA! HA! HA! HA!
HA! HA! HA!
QUIET NOW, LADS. A BET IS SERIOUS BUSINESS.
WHAT'S YOUR NAME, BOY?
ROBIN HOOD!
TELL ME THEN, ROBIN HOOD, WOULD YOU BE WILLING TO WAGER THAT PRETTY HORN YOU'RE BEARING AGAINST MY TEN SILVER MARKS?
WHAT, THIS? IT WAS A GIFT FROM MY UNCLE AND IS WORTH FAR MORE THAN THAT!
IF YOU'RE AFRAID YOU'RE NOT GOOD ENOUGH ...
HA! I CAN HIT ANY TARGET THAT WE CAN SEE FROM THIS SPOT!
IS THAT SO? THEN HIT ME THAT BUCK AT THE CLEARING'S EDGE.
HOLD ON, THAT'S ...
QUIET! LET THE BOY MAKE UP HIS MIND.

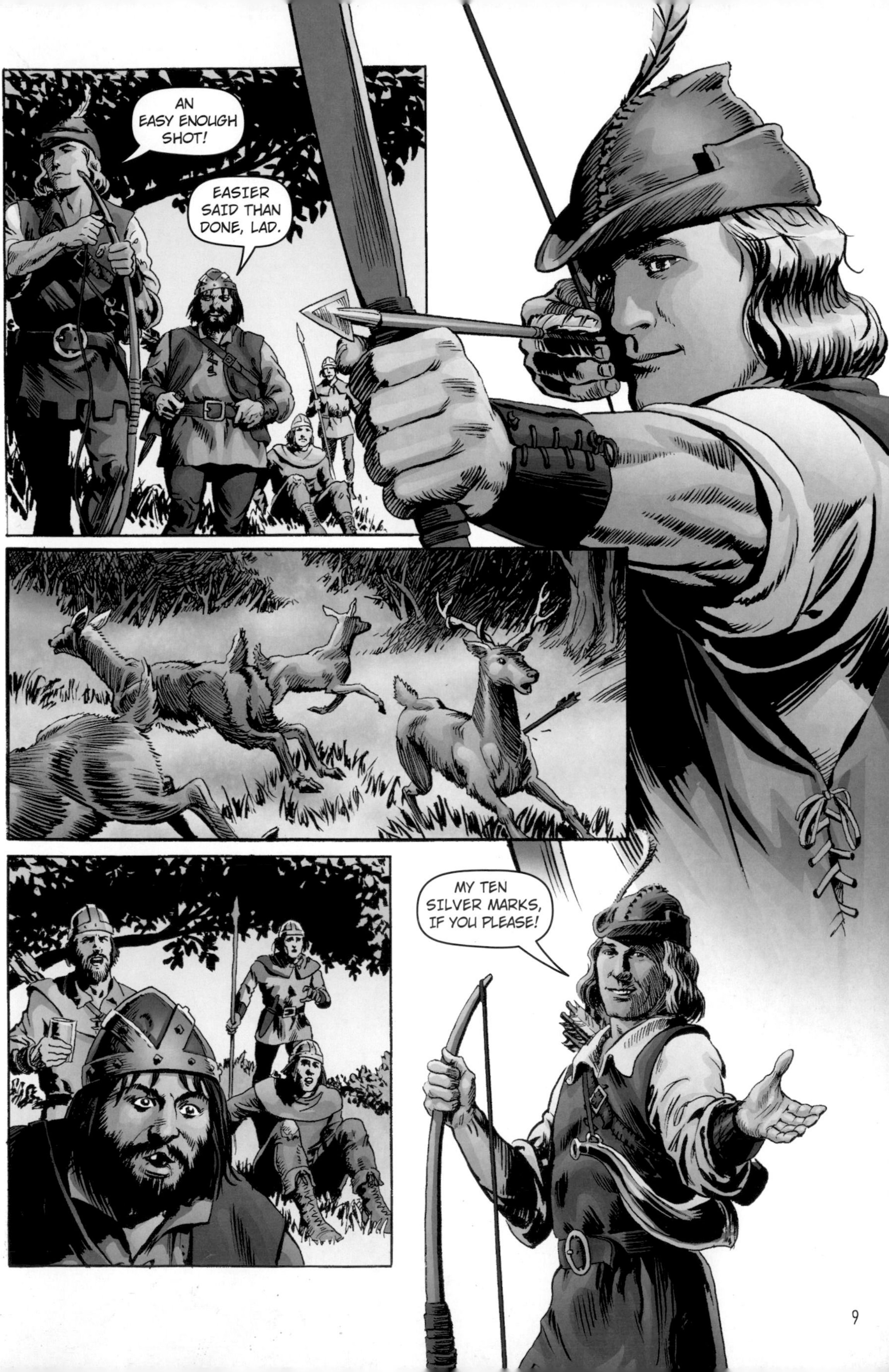
AN EASY ENOUGH SHOT!
EASIER SAID THAN DONE, LAD.
MY TEN SILVER MARKS, IF YOU PLEASE!

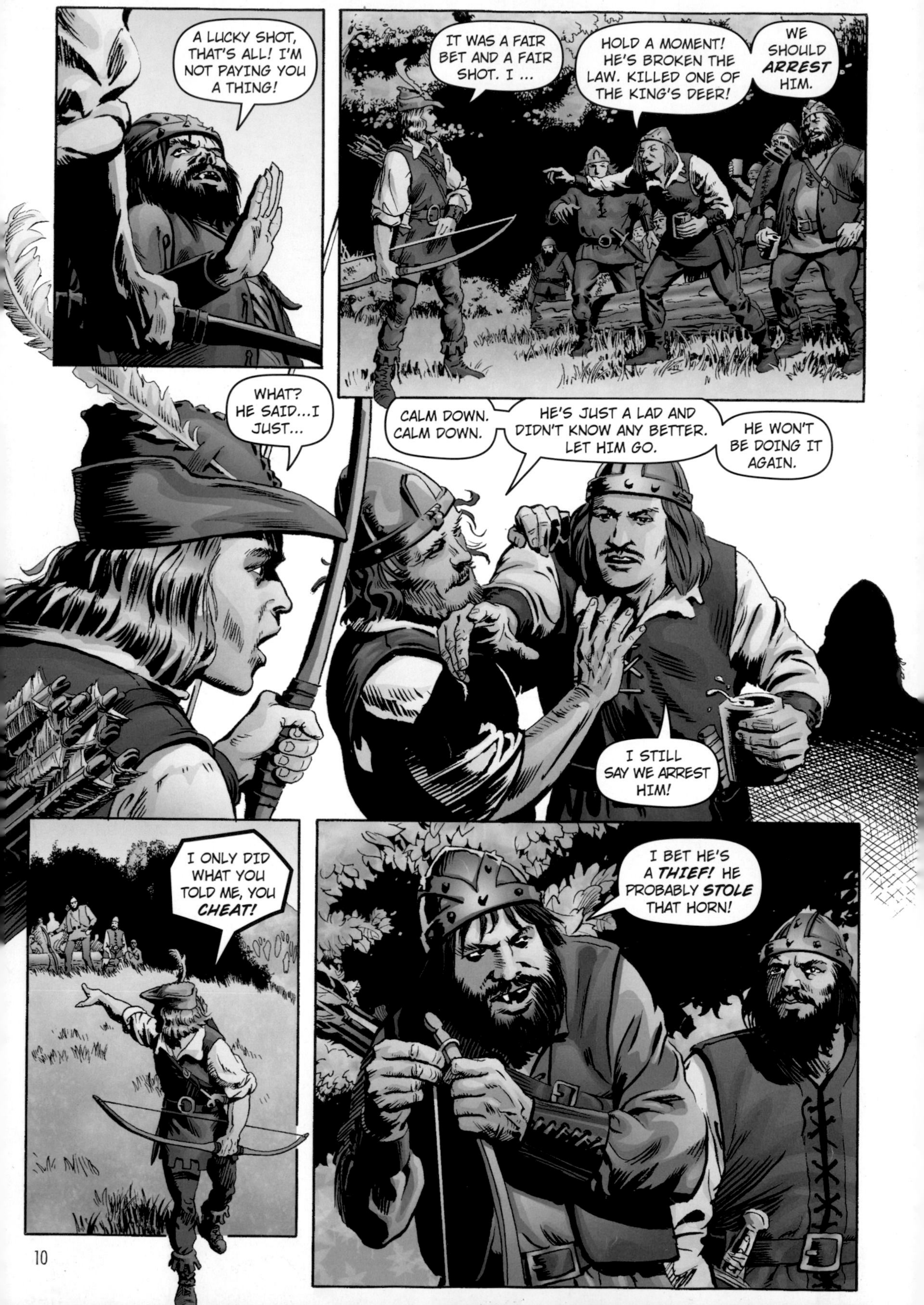
A LUCKY SHOT, THAT'S ALL! I'M NOT PAYING YOU A THING!
IT WAS A FAIR BET AND A FAIR SHOT. I ...
HOLD A MOMENT! HE'S BROKEN THE LAW. KILLED ONE OF THE KING'S DEER!
WE SHOULD ARREST HIM.
WHAT? HE SAID...I JUST...
CALM DOWN. CALM DOWN.
HE'S JUST A LAD AND DIDN'T KNOW ANY BETTER. LET HIM GO.
HE WON'T BE DOING IT AGAIN.
I STILL SAY WE ARREST HIM!
I ONLY DID WHAT YOU TOLD ME, YOU CHEAT!
I BET HE'S A THIEF! HE PROBABLY STOLE THAT HORN!

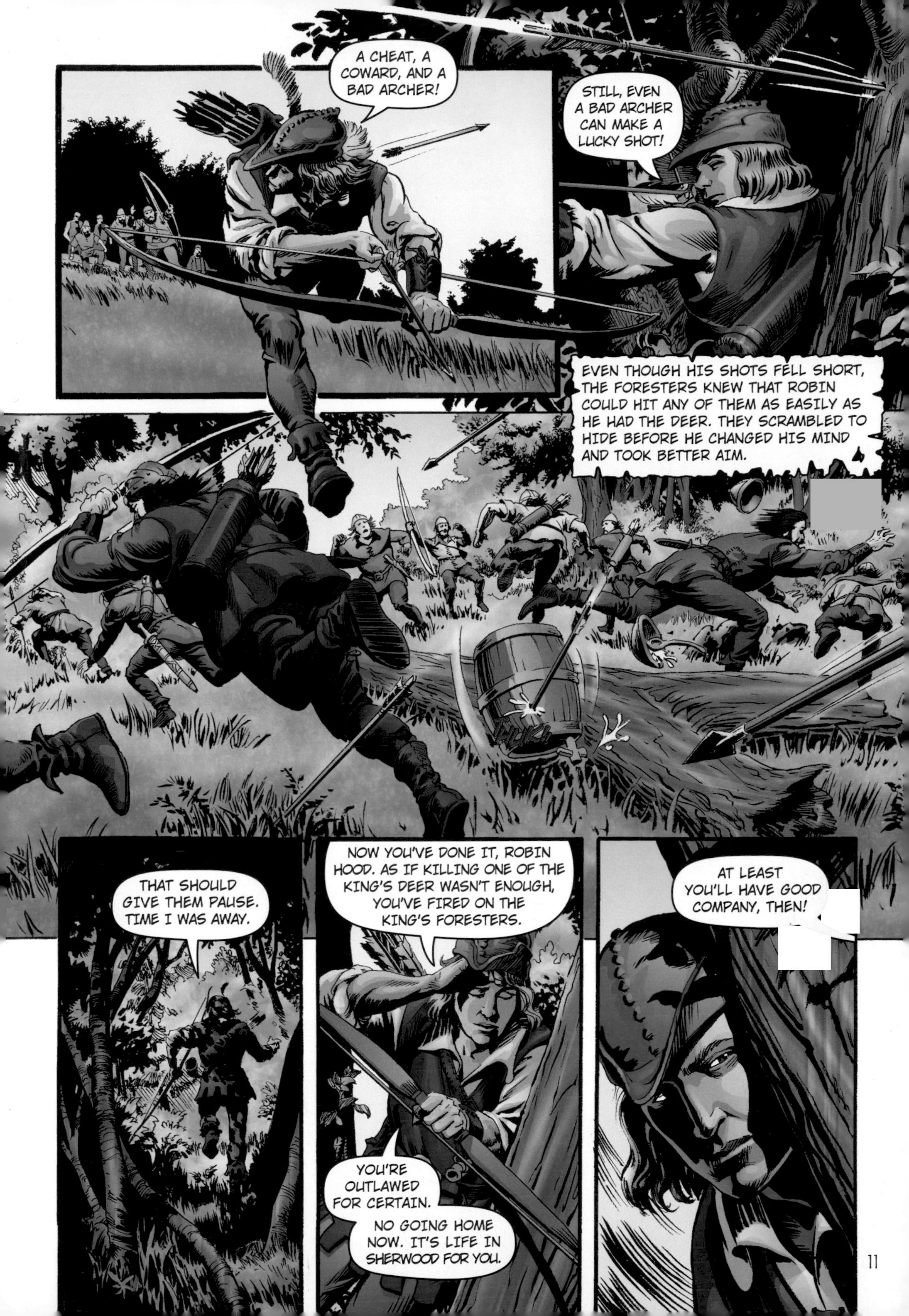
A CHEAT, A COWARD, AND A BAD ARCHER!
STILL, EVEN A BAD ARCHER CAN MAKE A LUCKY SHOT!
EVEN THOUGH HIS SHOTS FELL SHORT, THE FORESTERS KNEW THAT ROBIN COULD HIT ANY OF THEM AS EASILY AS HE HAD THE DEER. THEY SCRAMBLED TO HIDE BEFORE HE CHANGED HIS MIND AND TOOK BETTER AIM.
THUK!
THAT SHOULD GIVE THEM PAUSE. TIME I WAS AWAY.
NOW YOU'VE DONE IT, ROBIN HOOD. AS IF KILLING ONE OF THE KING'S DEER WASN'T ENOUGH, YOU'VE FIRED ON THE KING'S FORESTERS.
YOU'RE OUTLAWED FOR CERTAIN.
NO GOING HOME NOW. IT'S LIFE IN SHERWOOD FOR YOU.
AT LEAST YOU'LL HAVE GOOD COMPANY, THEN!

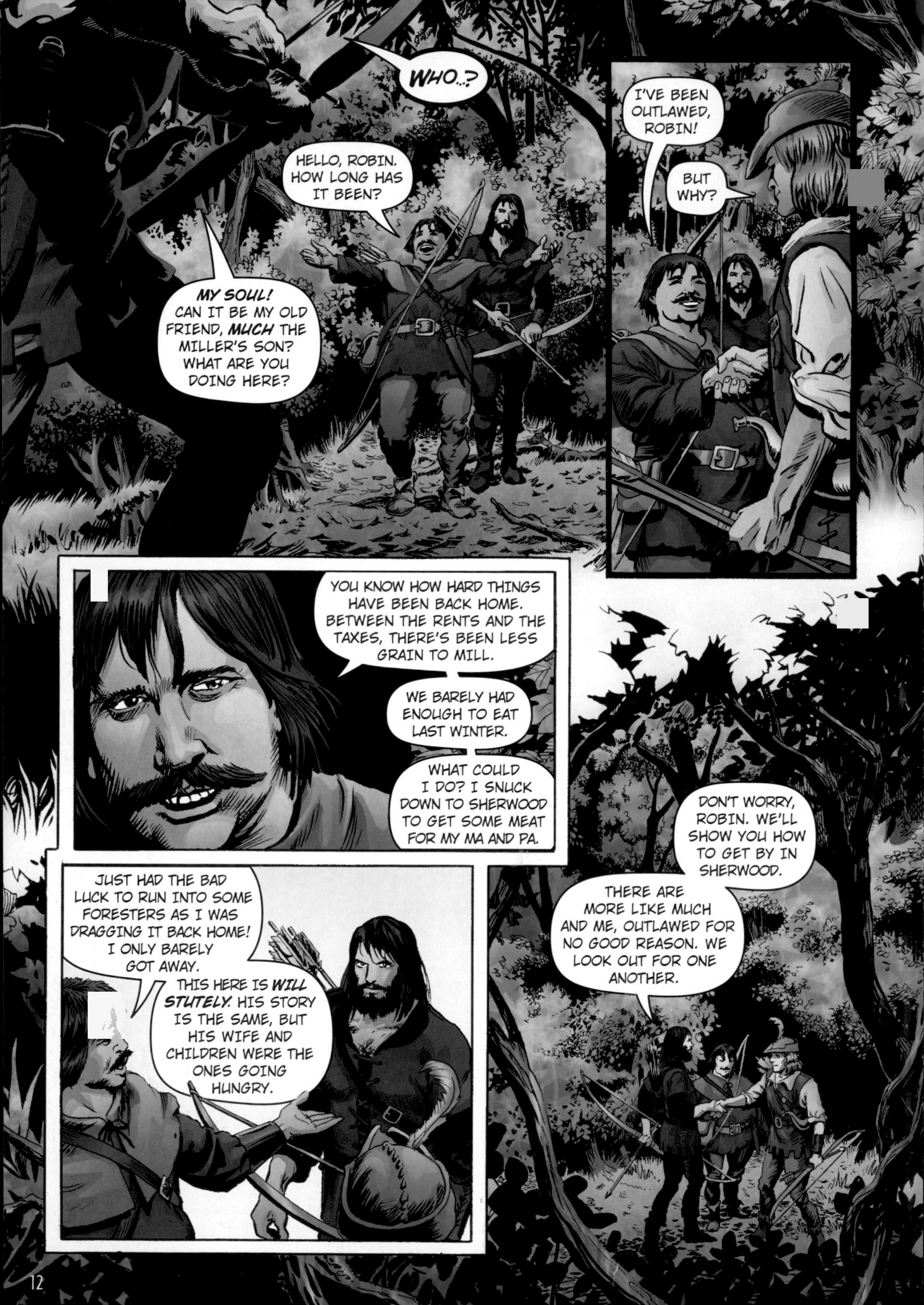
WHO..?
HELLO, ROBIN. HOW LONG HAS IT BEEN?
MY SOUL! CAN IT BE MY OLD FRIEND, MUCH THE MILLER'S SON? WHAT ARE YOU DOING HERE?
I'VE BEEN OUTLAWED, ROBIN!
BUT WHY?
YOU KNOW HOW HARD THINGS HAVE BEEN BACK HOME. BETWEEN THE RENTS AND THE TAXES, THERE'S BEEN LESS GRAIN TO MILL.
WE BARELY HAD ENOUGH TO EAT LAST WINTER.
WHAT COULD I DO? I SNUCK DOWN TO SHERWOOD TO GET SOME MEAT FOR MY MA AND PA.
JUST HAD THE BAD LUCK TO RUN INTO SOME FORESTERS AS I WAS DRAGGING IT BACK HOME! I ONLY BARELY GOT AWAY.
THIS HERE IS WILL STUTELY. HIS STORY IS THE SAME, BUT HIS WIFE AND CHILDREN WERE THE ONES GOING HUNGRY.
DON'T WORRY, ROBIN. WE'LL SHOW YOU HOW TO GET BY IN SHERWOOD.
THERE ARE MORE LIKE MUCH AND ME, OUTLAWED FOR NO GOOD REASON. WE LOOK OUT FOR ONE ANOTHER.

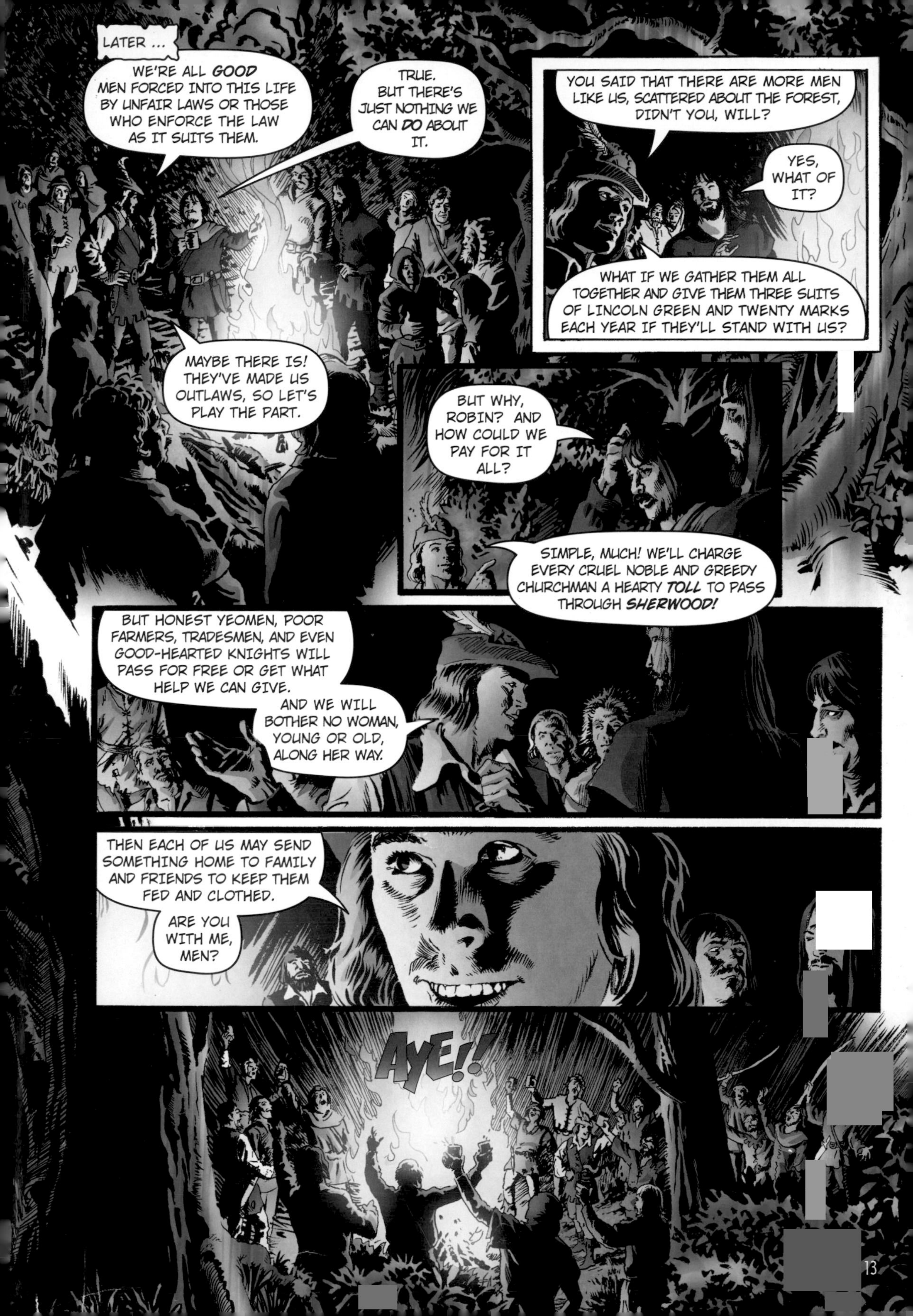

LATER ...
WE'RE ALL GOOD MEN FORCED INTO THIS LIFE BY UNFAIR LAWS OR THOSE WHO ENFORCE THE LAW AS IT SUITS THEM.
TRUE. BUT THERE'S JUST NOTHING WE CAN DO ABOUT IT.
MAYBE THERE IS! THEY'VE MADE US OUTLAWS, SO LET'S PLAY THE PART.
YOU SAID THAT THERE ARE MORE MEN LIKE US, SCATTERED ABOUT THE FOREST, DIDN'T YOU, WILL?
YES, WHAT OF IT?
WHAT IF WE GATHER THEM ALL TOGETHER AND GIVE THEM THREE SUITS OF LINCOLN GREEN AND TWENTY MARKS EACH YEAR IF THEY'LL STAND WITH US?
BUT WHY, ROBIN? AND HOW COULD WE PAY FOR IT ALL?
SIMPLE, MUCH! WE'LL CHARGE EVERY CRUEL NOBLE AND GREEDY CHURCHMAN A HEARTY TOLL TO PASS THROUGH SHERWOOD!
BUT HONEST YEOMEN, POOR FARMERS, TRADESMEN, AND EVEN GOOD-HEARTED KNIGHTS WILL PASS FOR FREE OR GET WHAT HELP WE CAN GIVE.
AND WE WILL BOTHER NO WOMAN, YOUNG OR OLD, ALONG HER WAY.
THEN EACH OF US MAY SEND SOMETHING HOME TO FAMILY AND FRIENDS TO KEEP THEM FED AND CLOTHED.
ARE YOU WITH ME, MEN?
AYE!!

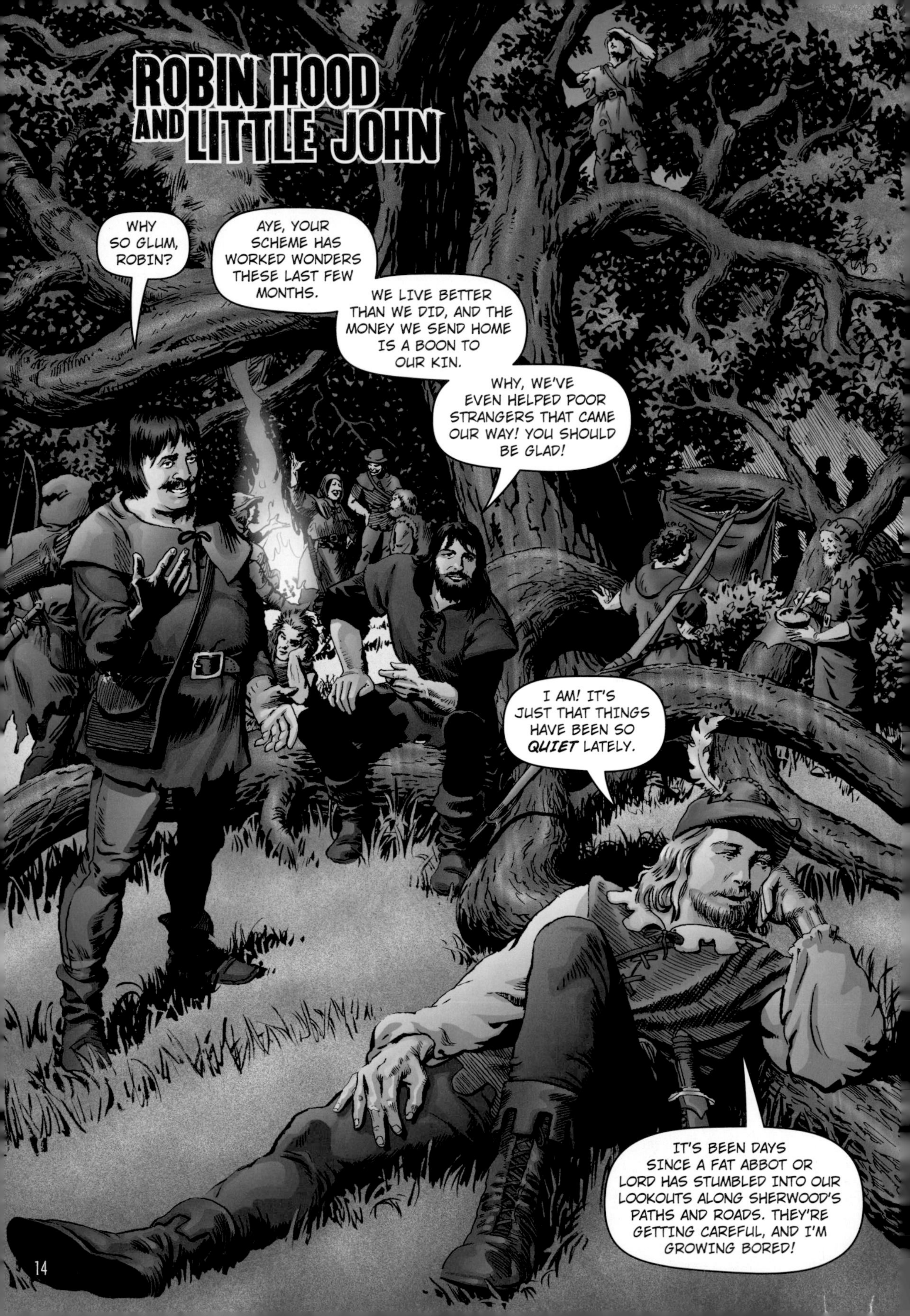
ROBIN HOOD AND LITTLE JOHN
WHY SO GLUM, ROBIN?
AYE, YOUR SCHEME HAS WORKED WONDERS THESE LAST FEW MONTHS.
WE LIVE BETTER THAN WE DID, AND THE MONEY WE SEND HOME IS A BOON TO OUR KIN.
WHY, WE'VE EVEN HELPED POOR STRANGERS THAT CAME OUR WAY! YOU SHOULD BE GLAD!
I AM! IT'S JUST THAT THINGS HAVE BEEN SO *QUIET* LATELY.
IT'S BEEN DAYS SINCE A FAT ABBOT OR LORD HAS STUMBLED INTO OUR LOOKOUTS ALONG SHERWOOD'S PATHS AND ROADS. THEY'RE GETTING CAREFUL, AND I'M GROWING BORED!

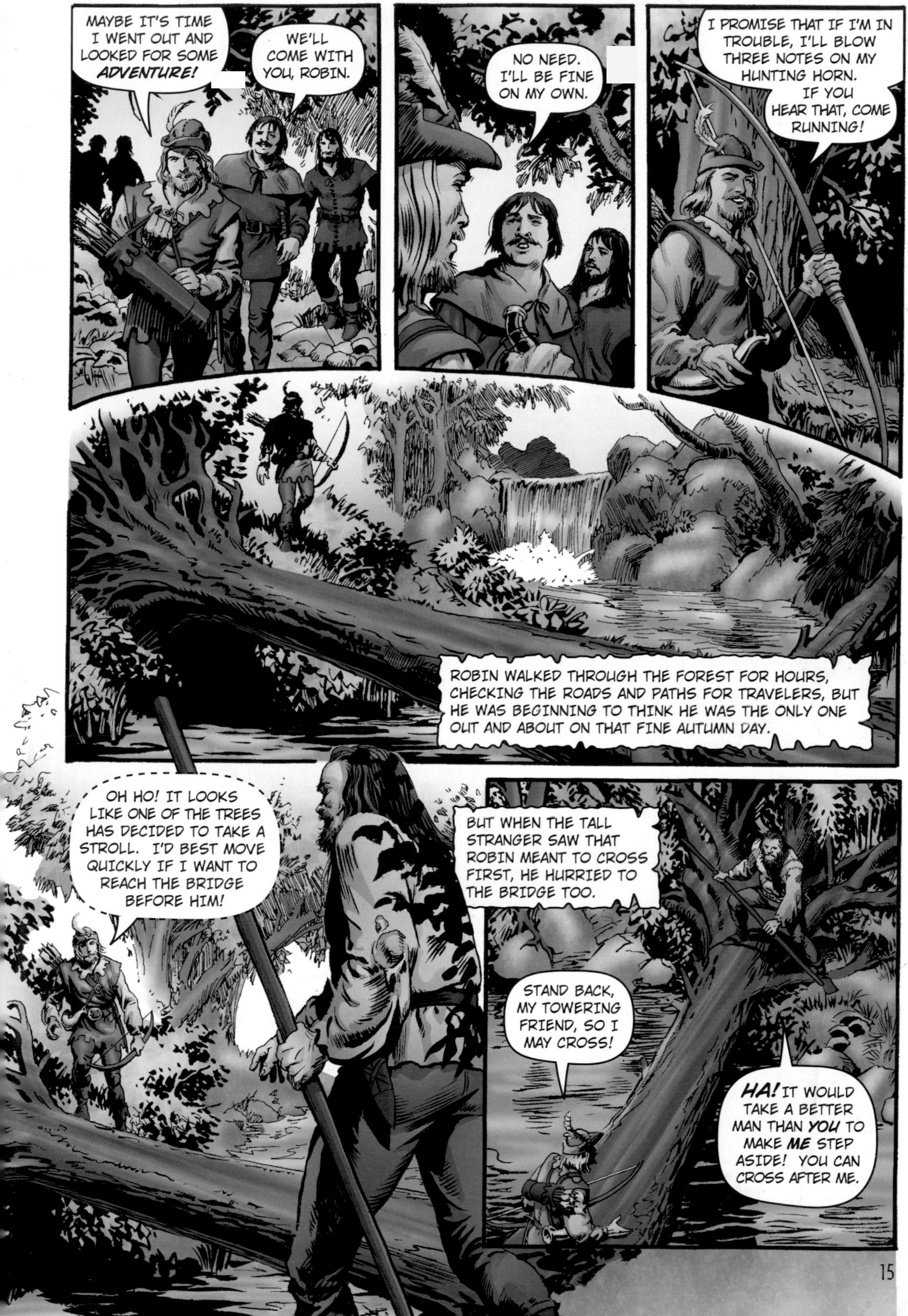

MAYBE IT'S TIME I WENT OUT AND LOOKED FOR SOME ADVENTURE!
WE'LL COME WITH YOU, ROBIN.
NO NEED. I'LL BE FINE ON MY OWN.
I PROMISE THAT IF I'M IN TROUBLE, I'LL BLOW THREE NOTES ON MY HUNTING HORN. IF YOU HEAR THAT, COME RUNNING!
ROBIN WALKED THROUGH THE FOREST FOR HOURS, CHECKING THE ROADS AND PATHS FOR TRAVELERS, BUT HE WAS BEGINNING TO THINK HE WAS THE ONLY ONE OUT AND ABOUT ON THAT FINE AUTUMN DAY.
OH HO! IT LOOKS LIKE ONE OF THE TREES HAS DECIDED TO TAKE A STROLL. I'D BEST MOVE QUICKLY IF I WANT TO REACH THE BRIDGE BEFORE HIM!
BUT WHEN THE TALL STRANGER SAW THAT ROBIN MEANT TO CROSS FIRST, HE HURRIED TO THE BRIDGE TOO.
STAND BACK, MY TOWERING FRIEND, SO I MAY CROSS!
HA! IT WOULD TAKE A BETTER MAN THAN YOU TO MAKE ME STEP ASIDE! YOU CAN CROSS AFTER ME.

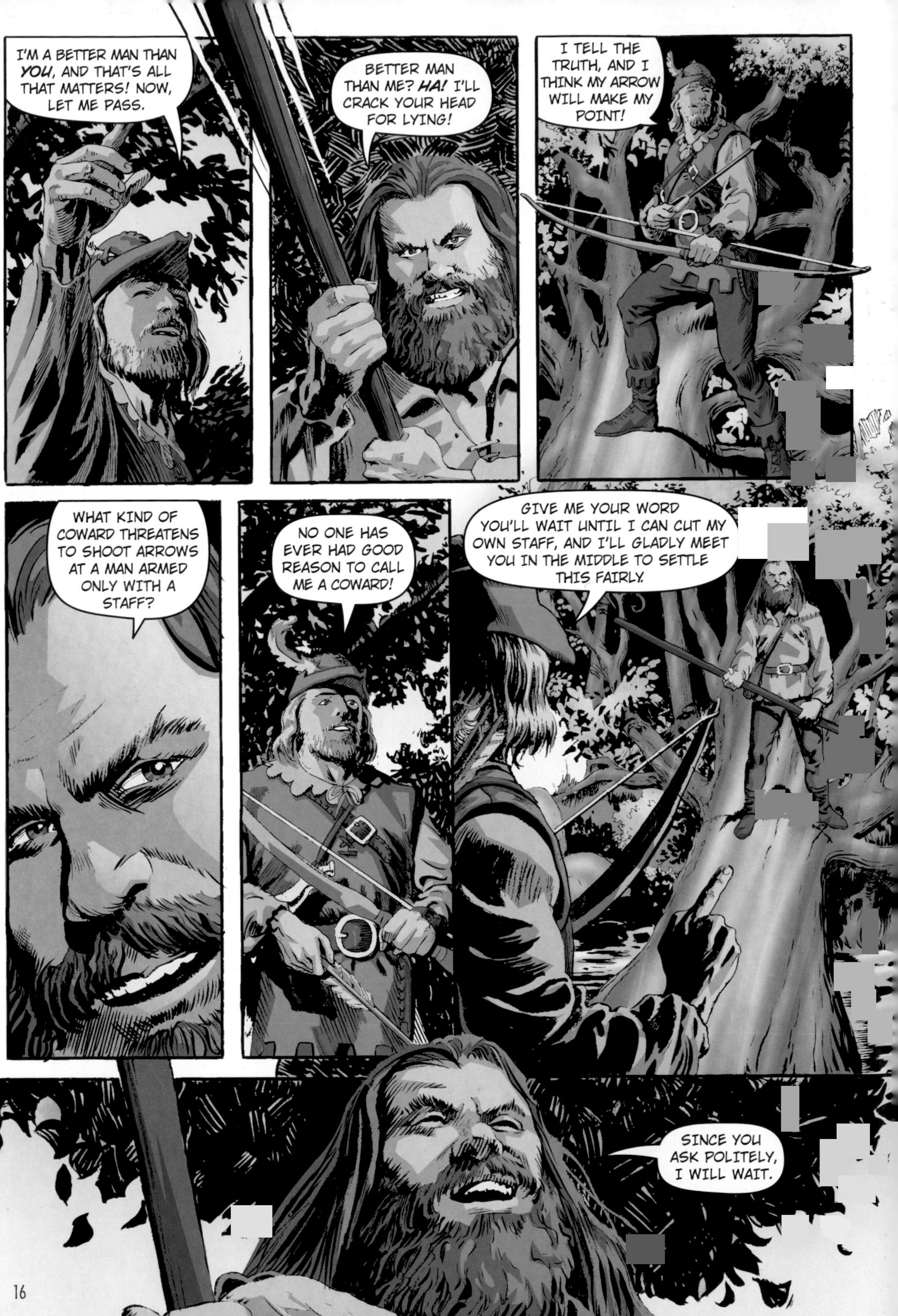
I'M A BETTER MAN THAN *YOU*, AND THAT'S ALL THAT MATTERS! NOW, LET ME PASS.
BETTER MAN THAN ME? *HA!* I'LL CRACK YOUR HEAD FOR LYING!
I TELL THE TRUTH, AND I THINK MY ARROW WILL MAKE MY POINT!
WHAT KIND OF COWARD THREATENS TO SHOOT ARROWS AT A MAN ARMED ONLY WITH A STAFF?
NO ONE HAS EVER HAD GOOD REASON TO CALL ME A COWARD!
GIVE ME YOUR WORD YOU'LL WAIT UNTIL I CAN CUT MY OWN STAFF, AND I'LL GLADLY MEET YOU IN THE MIDDLE TO SETTLE THIS FAIRLY.
SINCE YOU ASK POLITELY, I WILL WAIT.

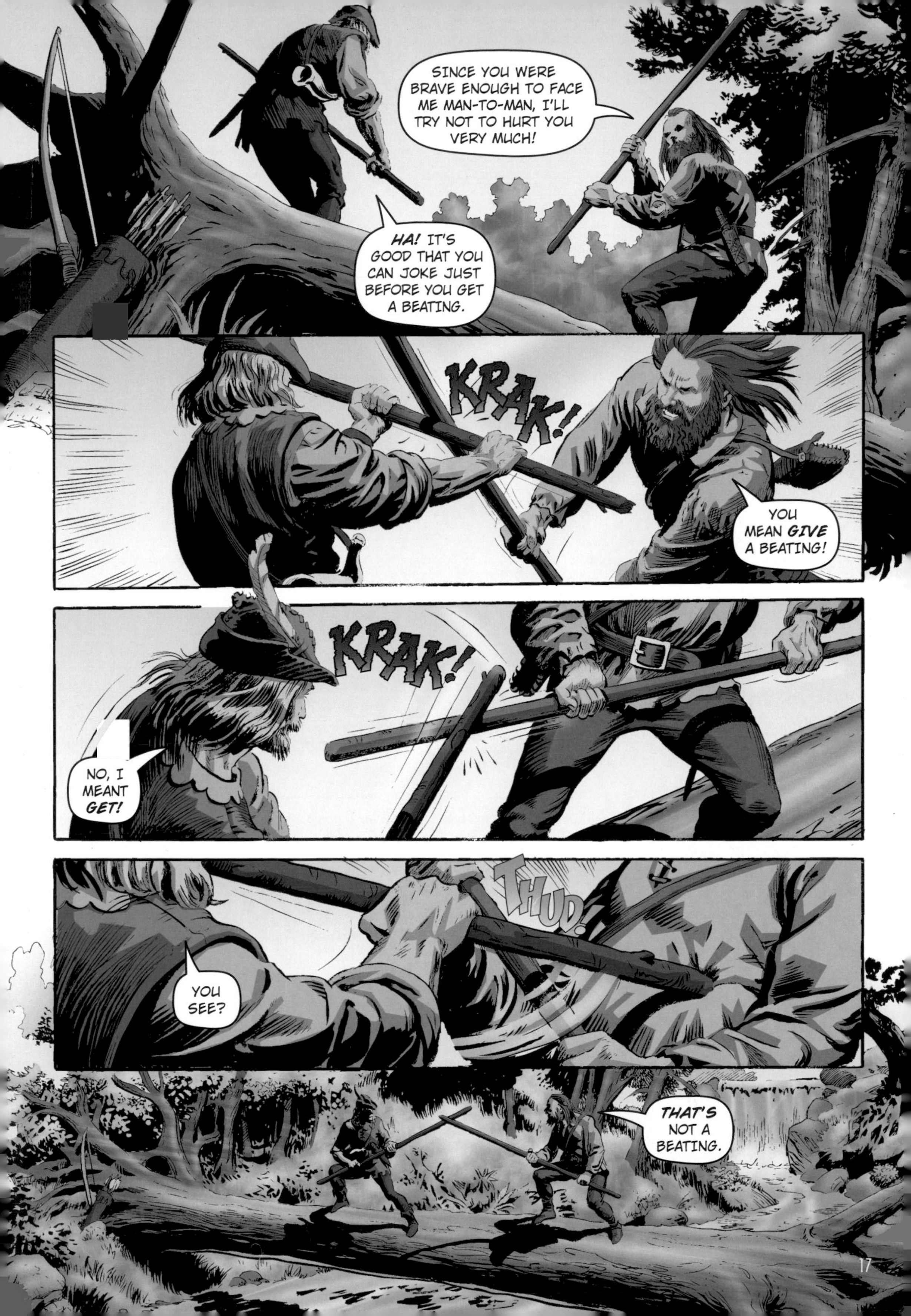
SINCE YOU WERE BRAVE ENOUGH TO FACE ME MAN-TO-MAN, I'LL TRY NOT TO HURT YOU VERY MUCH!
HA! IT'S GOOD THAT YOU CAN JOKE JUST BEFORE YOU GET A BEATING.
KRAK!
YOU MEAN *GIVE* A BEATING!
KRAK!
NO, I MEANT *GET!*
THUD!
YOU SEE?
THAT'S NOT A BEATING.

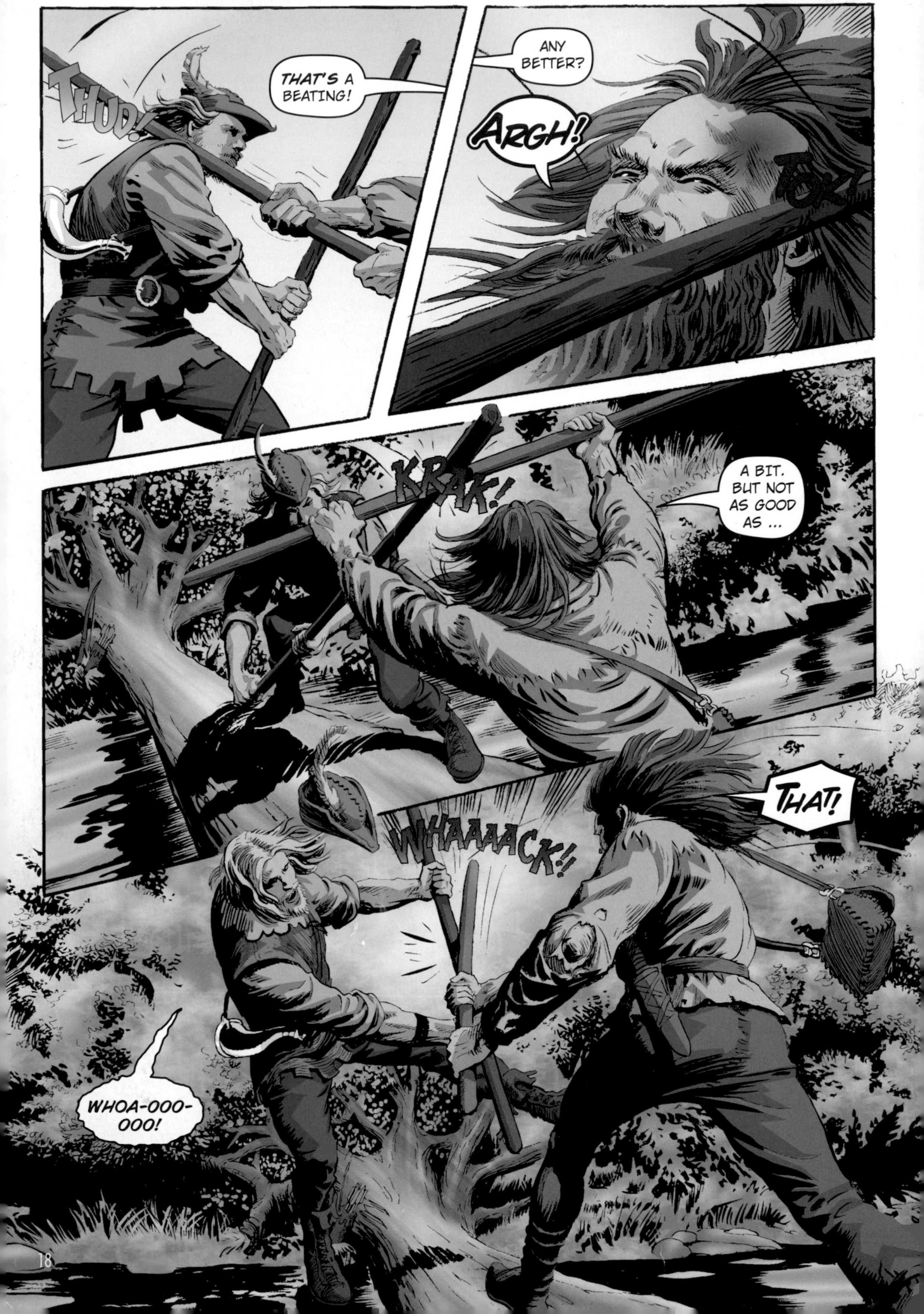
THUD!
THAT'S A BEATING!
ANY BETTER?
ARGH!
TOK!
KRAK!
A BIT. BUT NOT AS GOOD AS ...
THAT!
WHAAAACK!!
WHOA-OOO-OOO!

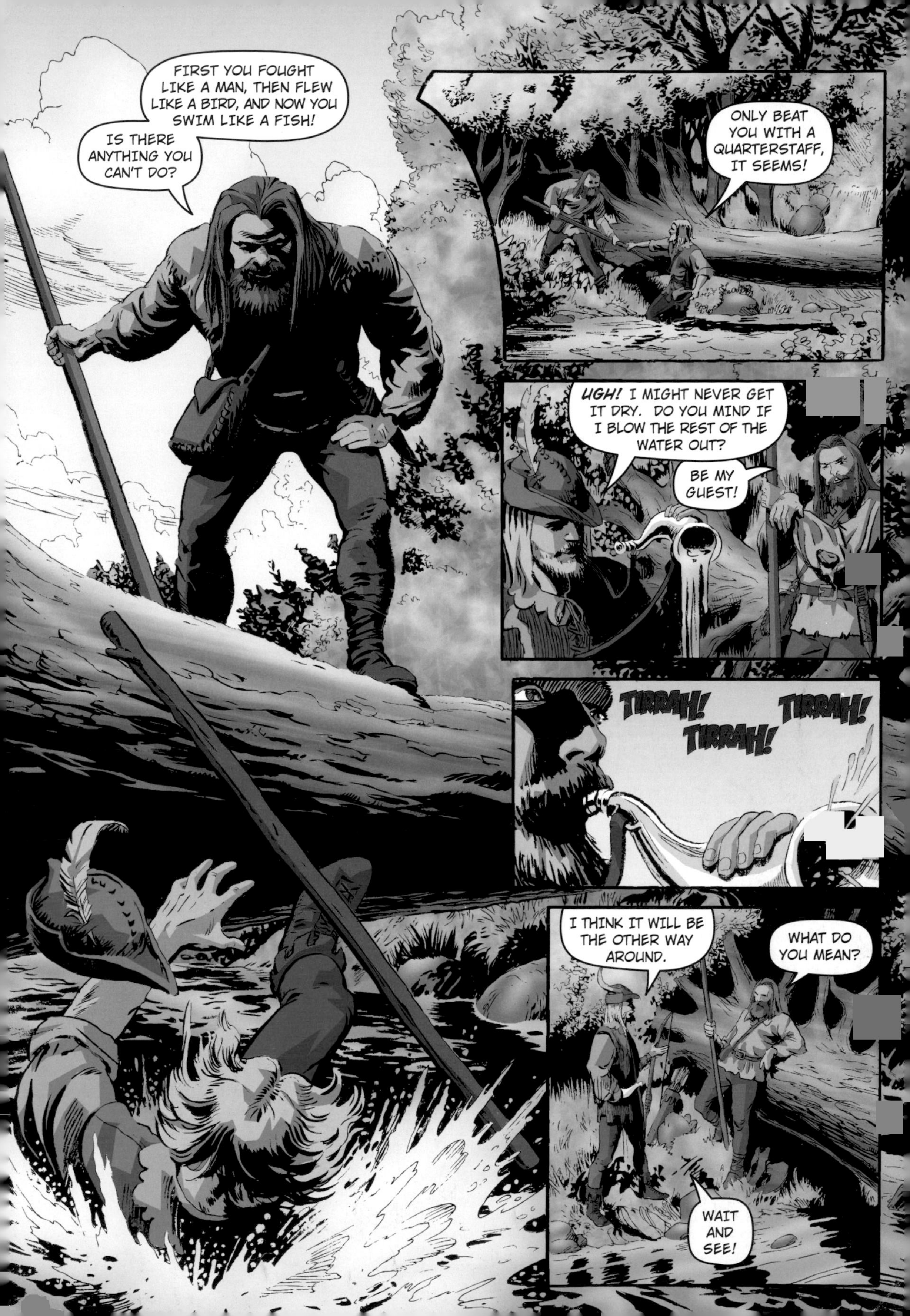
FIRST YOU FOUGHT LIKE A MAN, THEN FLEW LIKE A BIRD, AND NOW YOU SWIM LIKE A FISH!
IS THERE ANYTHING YOU CAN'T DO?
ONLY BEAT YOU WITH A QUARTERSTAFF, IT SEEMS!
UGH! I MIGHT NEVER GET IT DRY. DO YOU MIND IF I BLOW THE REST OF THE WATER OUT?
BE MY GUEST!
TIRRAH!
TIRRAH!
TIRRAH!
I THINK IT WILL BE THE OTHER WAY AROUND.
WHAT DO YOU MEAN?
WAIT AND SEE!

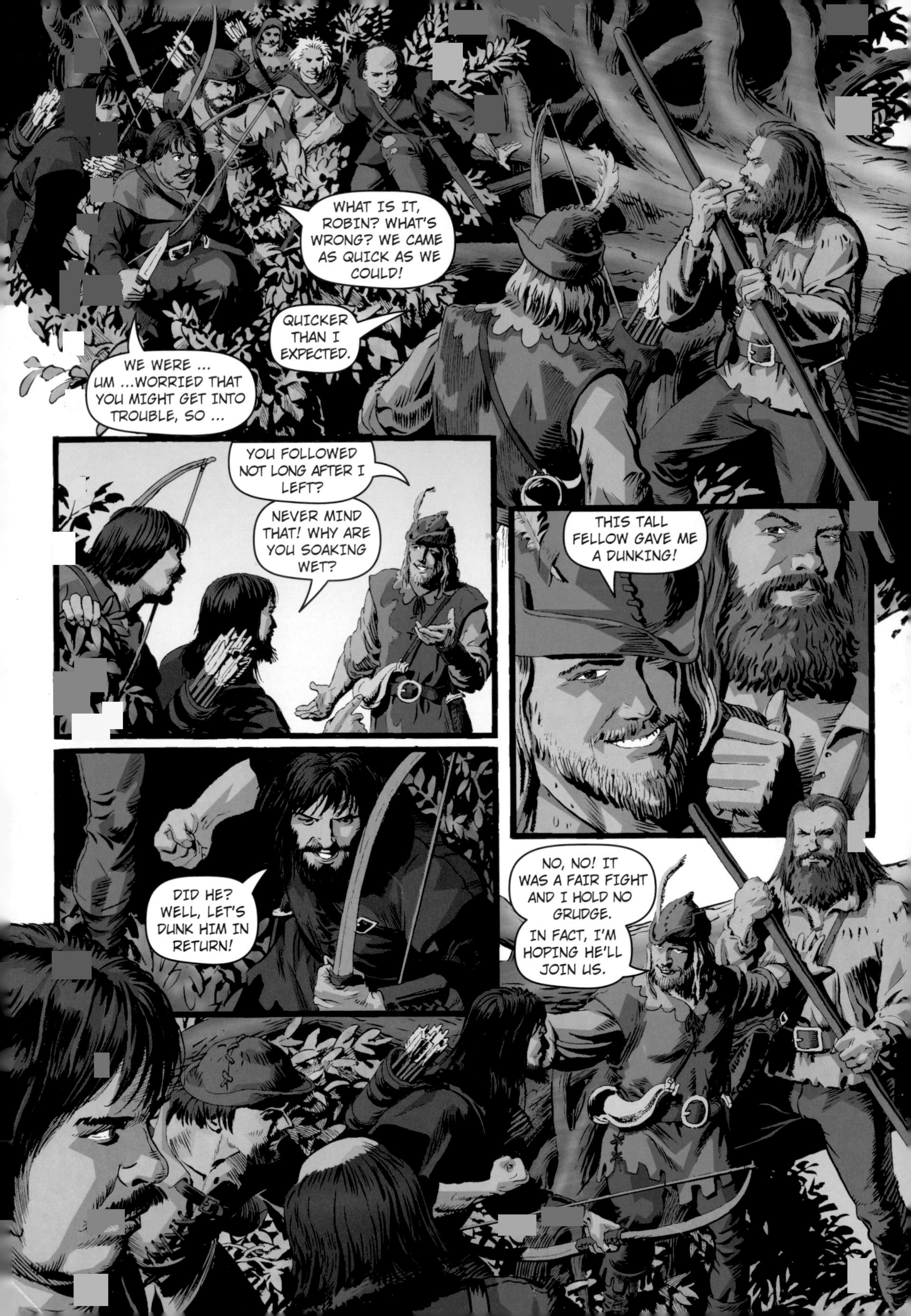

WHAT IS IT, ROBIN? WHAT'S WRONG? WE CAME AS QUICK AS WE COULD!
QUICKER THAN I EXPECTED.
WE WERE ... UM ...WORRIED THAT YOU MIGHT GET INTO TROUBLE, SO ...
YOU FOLLOWED NOT LONG AFTER I LEFT?
NEVER MIND THAT! WHY ARE YOU SOAKING WET?
THIS TALL FELLOW GAVE ME A DUNKING!
DID HE? WELL, LET'S DUNK HIM IN RETURN!
NO, NO! IT WAS A FAIR FIGHT AND I HOLD NO GRUDGE.
IN FACT, I'M HOPING HE'LL JOIN US.

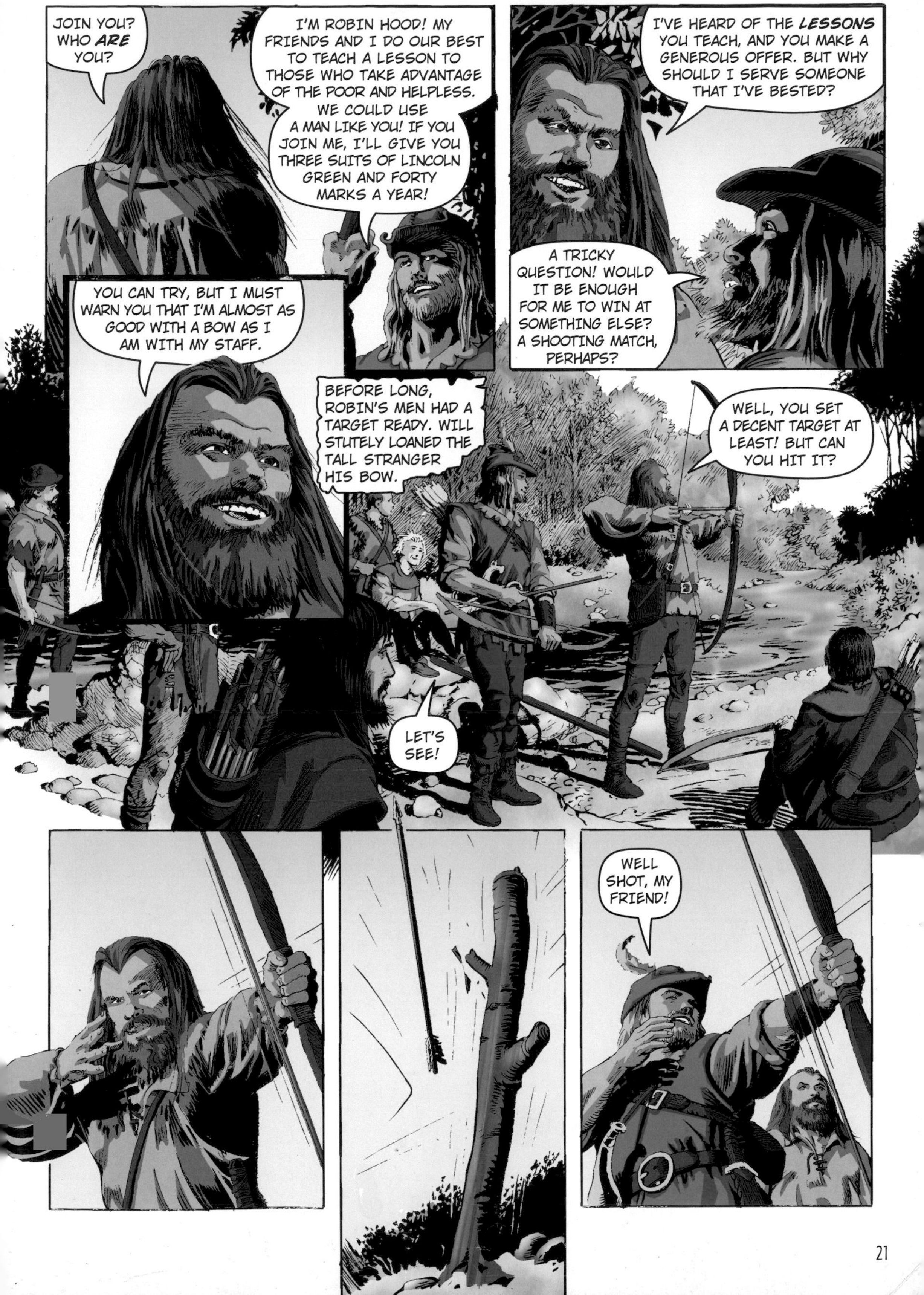

JOIN YOU? WHO *ARE* YOU?
I'M ROBIN HOOD! MY FRIENDS AND I DO OUR BEST TO TEACH A LESSON TO THOSE WHO TAKE ADVANTAGE OF THE POOR AND HELPLESS. WE COULD USE A MAN LIKE YOU! IF YOU JOIN ME, I'LL GIVE YOU THREE SUITS OF LINCOLN GREEN AND FORTY MARKS A YEAR!
I'VE HEARD OF THE *LESSONS* YOU TEACH, AND YOU MAKE A GENEROUS OFFER. BUT WHY SHOULD I SERVE SOMEONE THAT I'VE BESTED?
A TRICKY QUESTION! WOULD IT BE ENOUGH FOR ME TO WIN AT SOMETHING ELSE? A SHOOTING MATCH, PERHAPS?
YOU CAN TRY, BUT I MUST WARN YOU THAT I'M ALMOST AS GOOD WITH A BOW AS I AM WITH MY STAFF.
BEFORE LONG, ROBIN'S MEN HAD A TARGET READY. WILL STUTELY LOANED THE TALL STRANGER HIS BOW.
WELL, YOU SET A DECENT TARGET AT LEAST! BUT CAN YOU HIT IT?
LET'S SEE!
WELL SHOT, MY FRIEND!

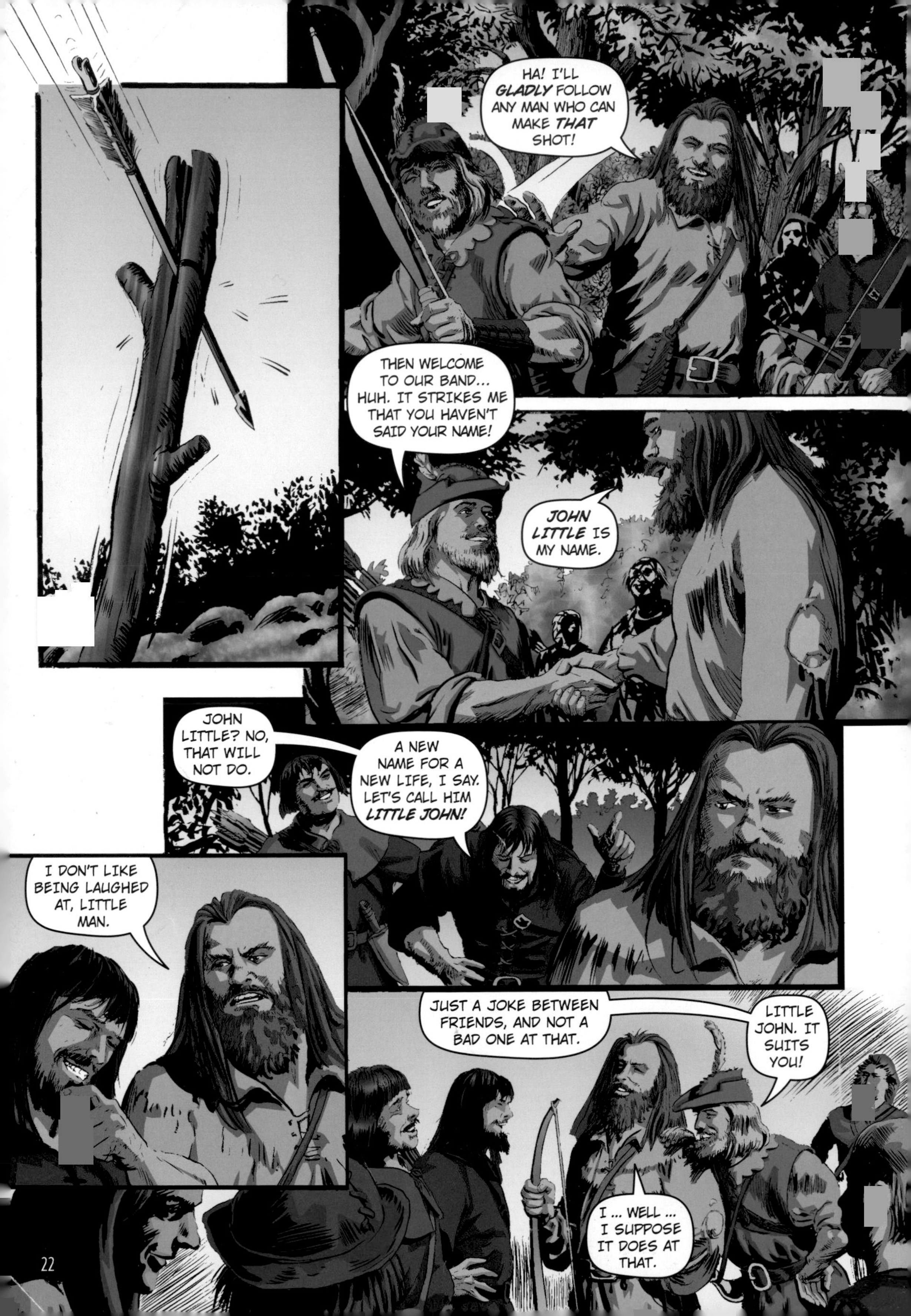
HA! I'LL GLADLY FOLLOW ANY MAN WHO CAN MAKE THAT SHOT!
THEN WELCOME TO OUR BAND... HUH. IT STRIKES ME THAT YOU HAVEN'T SAID YOUR NAME!
JOHN LITTLE IS MY NAME.
JOHN LITTLE? NO, THAT WILL NOT DO.
A NEW NAME FOR A NEW LIFE, I SAY. LET'S CALL HIM LITTLE JOHN!
I DON'T LIKE BEING LAUGHED AT, LITTLE MAN.
JUST A JOKE BETWEEN FRIENDS, AND NOT A BAD ONE AT THAT.
LITTLE JOHN. IT SUITS YOU!
I ... WELL ... I SUPPOSE IT DOES AT THAT.

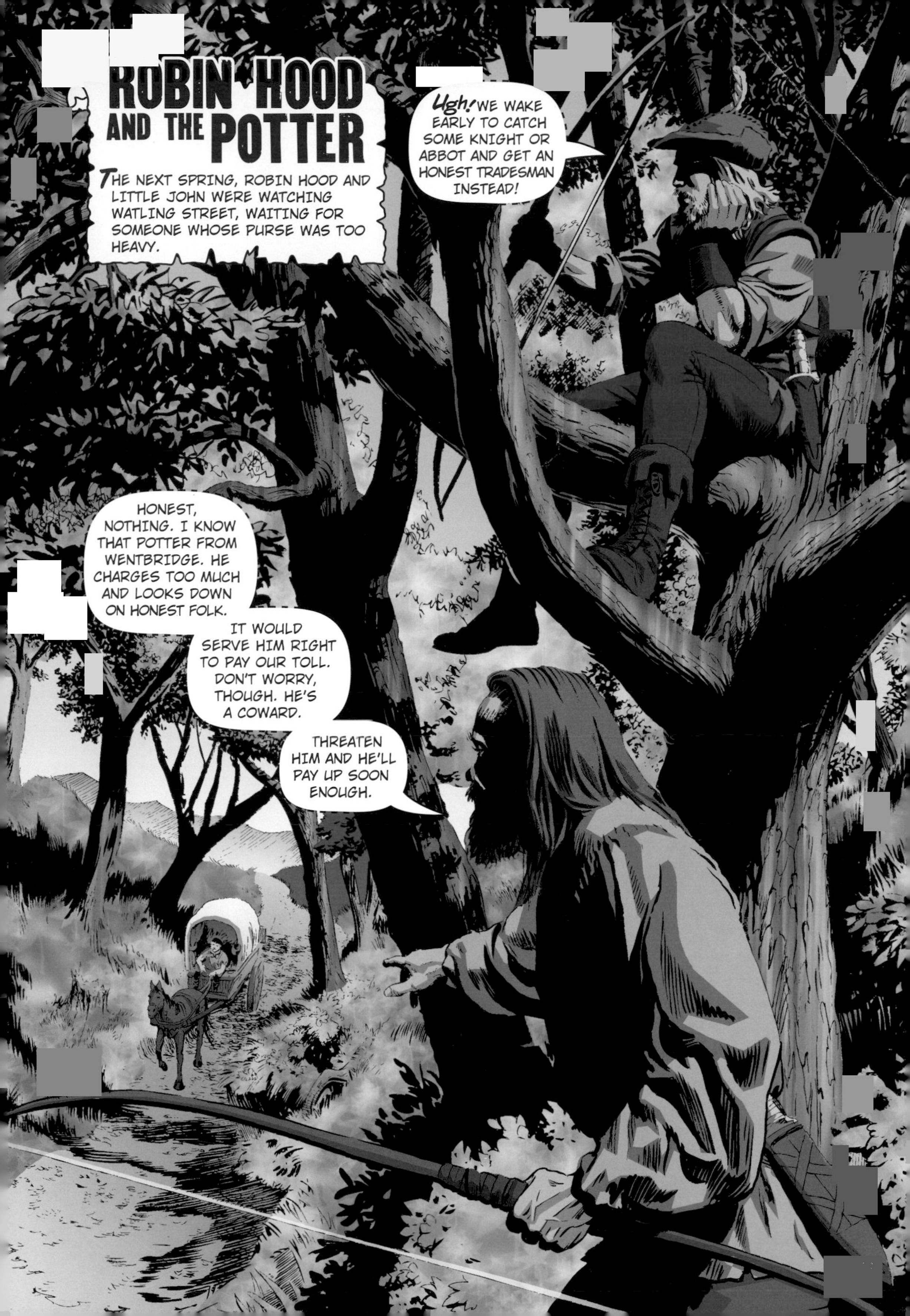
ROBIN HOOD AND THE POTTER
THE NEXT SPRING, ROBIN HOOD AND LITTLE JOHN WERE WATCHING WATLING STREET, WAITING FOR SOMEONE WHOSE PURSE WAS TOO HEAVY.
Ugh! WE WAKE EARLY TO CATCH SOME KNIGHT OR ABBOT AND GET AN HONEST TRADESMAN INSTEAD!
HONEST, NOTHING. I KNOW THAT POTTER FROM WENTBRIDGE. HE CHARGES TOO MUCH AND LOOKS DOWN ON HONEST FOLK.
IT WOULD SERVE HIM RIGHT TO PAY OUR TOLL. DON'T WORRY, THOUGH. HE'S A COWARD.
THREATEN HIM AND HE'LL PAY UP SOON ENOUGH.

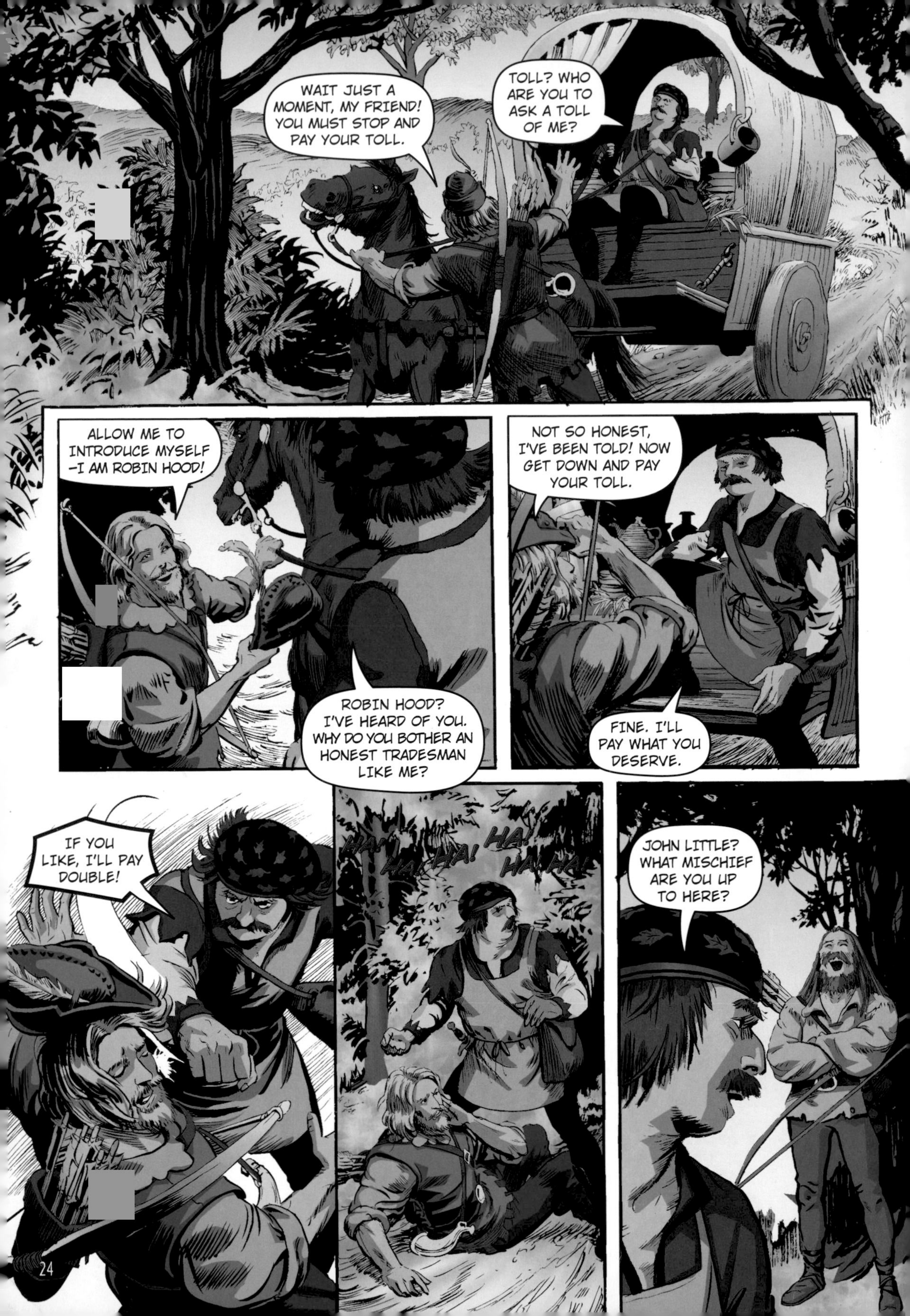

WAIT JUST A MOMENT, MY FRIEND! YOU MUST STOP AND PAY YOUR TOLL.
TOLL? WHO ARE YOU TO ASK A TOLL OF ME?
ALLOW ME TO INTRODUCE MYSELF –I AM ROBIN HOOD!
ROBIN HOOD? I'VE HEARD OF YOU. WHY DO YOU BOTHER AN HONEST TRADESMAN LIKE ME?
NOT SO HONEST, I'VE BEEN TOLD! NOW GET DOWN AND PAY YOUR TOLL.
FINE. I'LL PAY WHAT YOU DESERVE.
IF YOU LIKE, I'LL PAY DOUBLE!
HA! HA! HA!
HA! HA! HA!
JOHN LITTLE? WHAT MISCHIEF ARE YOU UP TO HERE?

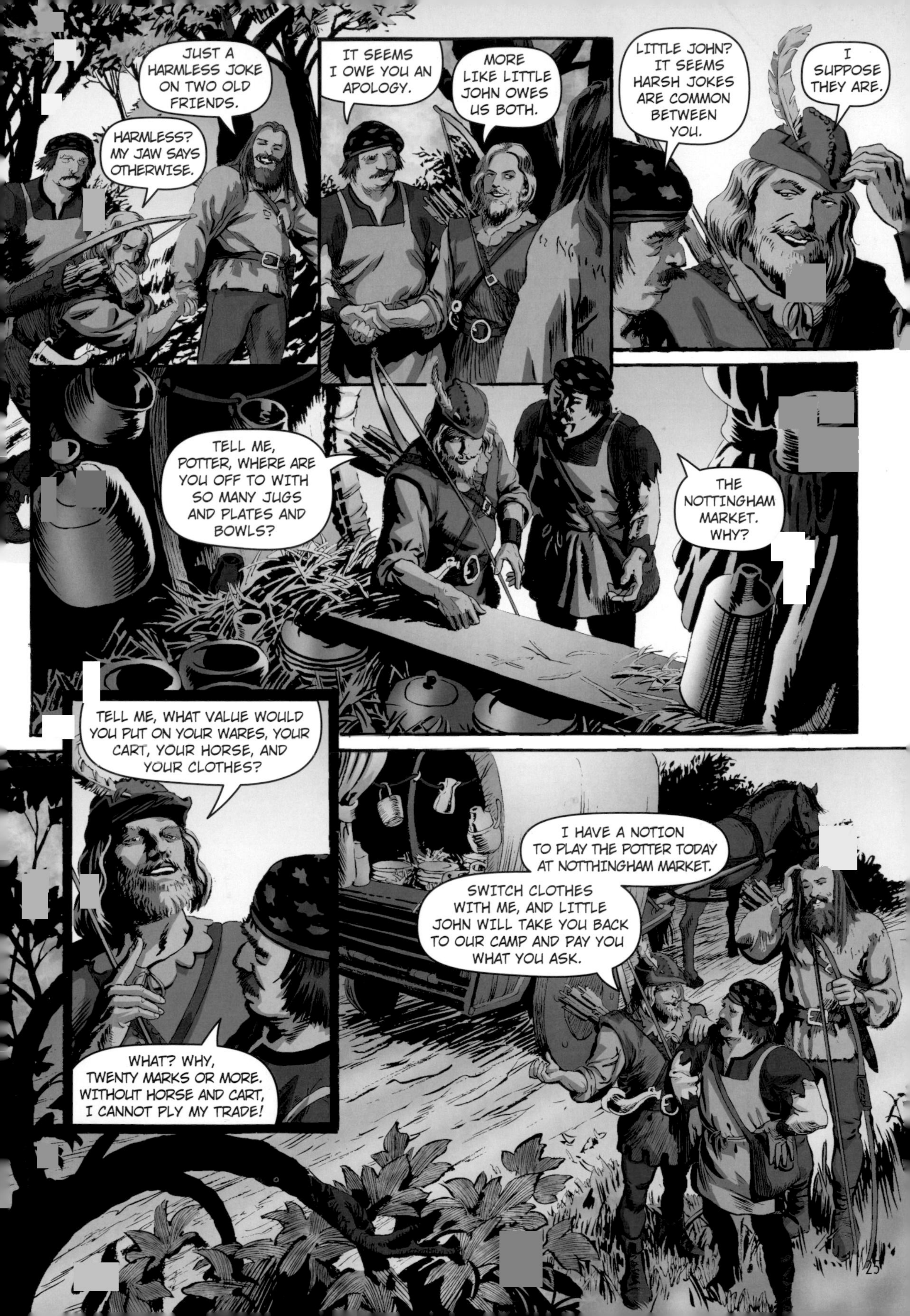
JUST A HARMLESS JOKE ON TWO OLD FRIENDS.
HARMLESS? MY JAW SAYS OTHERWISE.
IT SEEMS I OWE YOU AN APOLOGY.
MORE LIKE LITTLE JOHN OWES US BOTH.
LITTLE JOHN? IT SEEMS HARSH JOKES ARE COMMON BETWEEN YOU.
I SUPPOSE THEY ARE.
TELL ME, POTTER, WHERE ARE YOU OFF TO WITH SO MANY JUGS AND PLATES AND BOWLS?
THE NOTTINGHAM MARKET. WHY?
TELL ME, WHAT VALUE WOULD YOU PUT ON YOUR WARES, YOUR CART, YOUR HORSE, AND YOUR CLOTHES?
WHAT? WHY, TWENTY MARKS OR MORE. WITHOUT HORSE AND CART, I CANNOT PLY MY TRADE!
I HAVE A NOTION TO PLAY THE POTTER TODAY AT NOTTHINGHAM MARKET.
SWITCH CLOTHES WITH ME, AND LITTLE JOHN WILL TAKE YOU BACK TO OUR CAMP AND PAY YOU WHAT YOU ASK.

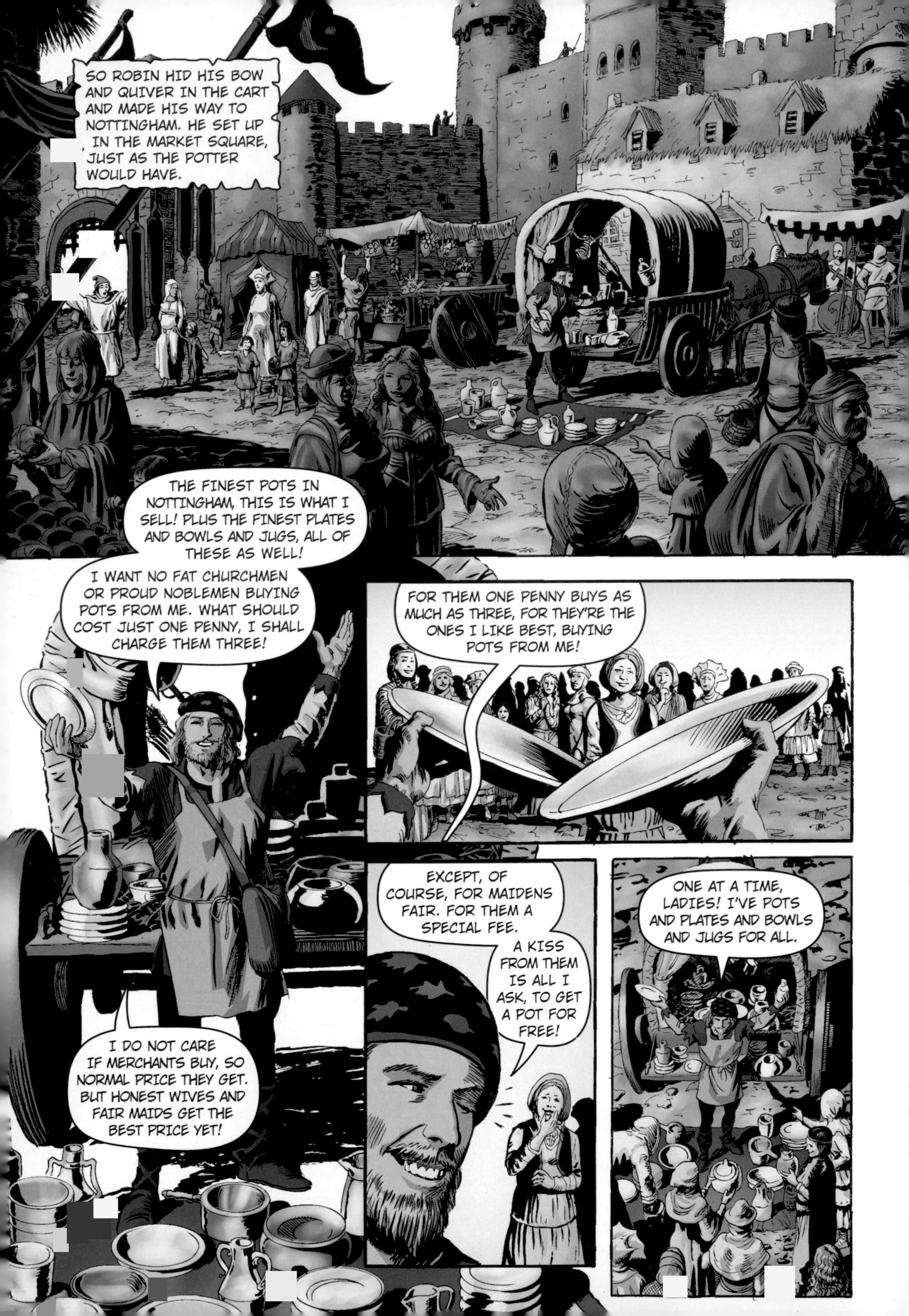
SO ROBIN HID HIS BOW AND QUIVER IN THE CART AND MADE HIS WAY TO NOTTINGHAM. HE SET UP IN THE MARKET SQUARE, JUST AS THE POTTER WOULD HAVE.
THE FINEST POTS IN NOTTINGHAM, THIS IS WHAT I SELL! PLUS THE FINEST PLATES AND BOWLS AND JUGS, ALL OF THESE AS WELL!
I WANT NO FAT CHURCHMEN OR PROUD NOBLEMEN BUYING POTS FROM ME. WHAT SHOULD COST JUST ONE PENNY, I SHALL CHARGE THEM THREE!
I DO NOT CARE IF MERCHANTS BUY, SO NORMAL PRICE THEY GET. BUT HONEST WIVES AND FAIR MAIDS GET THE BEST PRICE YET!
FOR THEM ONE PENNY BUYS AS MUCH AS THREE, FOR THEY'RE THE ONES I LIKE BEST, BUYING POTS FROM ME!
EXCEPT, OF COURSE, FOR MAIDENS FAIR. FOR THEM A SPECIAL FEE.
A KISS FROM THEM IS ALL I ASK, TO GET A POT FOR FREE!
ONE AT A TIME, LADIES! I'VE POTS AND PLATES AND BOWLS AND JUGS FOR ALL.

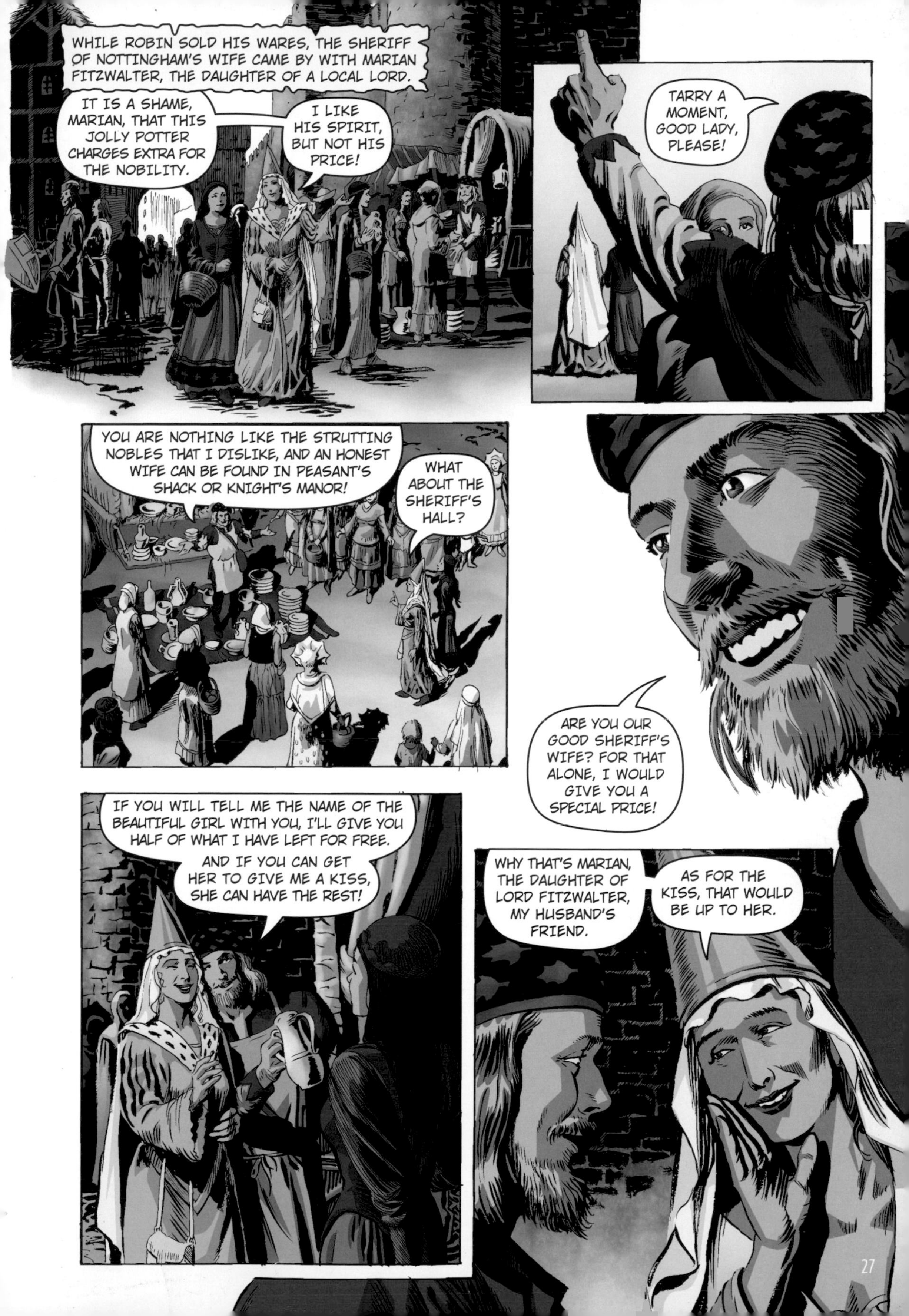

WHILE ROBIN SOLD HIS WARES, THE SHERIFF OF NOTTINGHAM'S WIFE CAME BY WITH MARIAN FITZWALTER, THE DAUGHTER OF A LOCAL LORD.
IT IS A SHAME, MARIAN, THAT THIS JOLLY POTTER CHARGES EXTRA FOR THE NOBILITY.
I LIKE HIS SPIRIT, BUT NOT HIS PRICE!
TARRY A MOMENT, GOOD LADY, PLEASE!
YOU ARE NOTHING LIKE THE STRUTTING NOBLES THAT I DISLIKE, AND AN HONEST WIFE CAN BE FOUND IN PEASANT'S SHACK OR KNIGHT'S MANOR!
WHAT ABOUT THE SHERIFF'S HALL?
ARE YOU OUR GOOD SHERIFF'S WIFE? FOR THAT ALONE, I WOULD GIVE YOU A SPECIAL PRICE!
IF YOU WILL TELL ME THE NAME OF THE BEAUTIFUL GIRL WITH YOU, I'LL GIVE YOU HALF OF WHAT I HAVE LEFT FOR FREE.
AND IF YOU CAN GET HER TO GIVE ME A KISS, SHE CAN HAVE THE REST!
WHY THAT'S MARIAN, THE DAUGHTER OF LORD FITZWALTER, MY HUSBAND'S FRIEND.
AS FOR THE KISS, THAT WOULD BE UP TO HER.

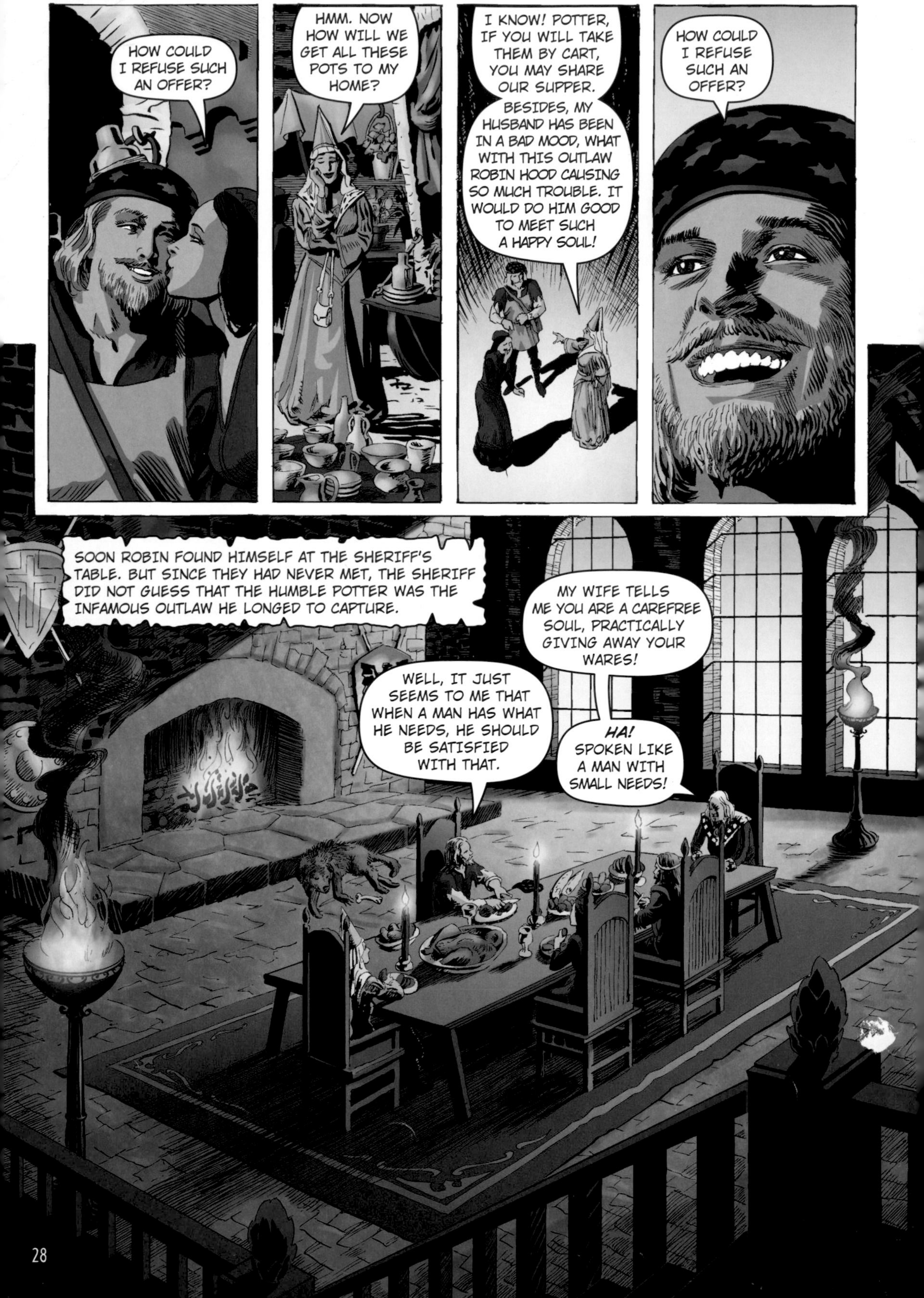
HOW COULD I REFUSE SUCH AN OFFER?
HMM. NOW HOW WILL WE GET ALL THESE POTS TO MY HOME?
I KNOW! POTTER, IF YOU WILL TAKE THEM BY CART, YOU MAY SHARE OUR SUPPER.
BESIDES, MY HUSBAND HAS BEEN IN A BAD MOOD, WHAT WITH THIS OUTLAW ROBIN HOOD CAUSING SO MUCH TROUBLE. IT WOULD DO HIM GOOD TO MEET SUCH A HAPPY SOUL!
HOW COULD I REFUSE SUCH AN OFFER?
SOON ROBIN FOUND HIMSELF AT THE SHERIFF'S TABLE. BUT SINCE THEY HAD NEVER MET, THE SHERIFF DID NOT GUESS THAT THE HUMBLE POTTER WAS THE INFAMOUS OUTLAW HE LONGED TO CAPTURE.
MY WIFE TELLS ME YOU ARE A CAREFREE SOUL, PRACTICALLY GIVING AWAY YOUR WARES!
WELL, IT JUST SEEMS TO ME THAT WHEN A MAN HAS WHAT HE NEEDS, HE SHOULD BE SATISFIED WITH THAT.
HA! SPOKEN LIKE A MAN WITH SMALL NEEDS!

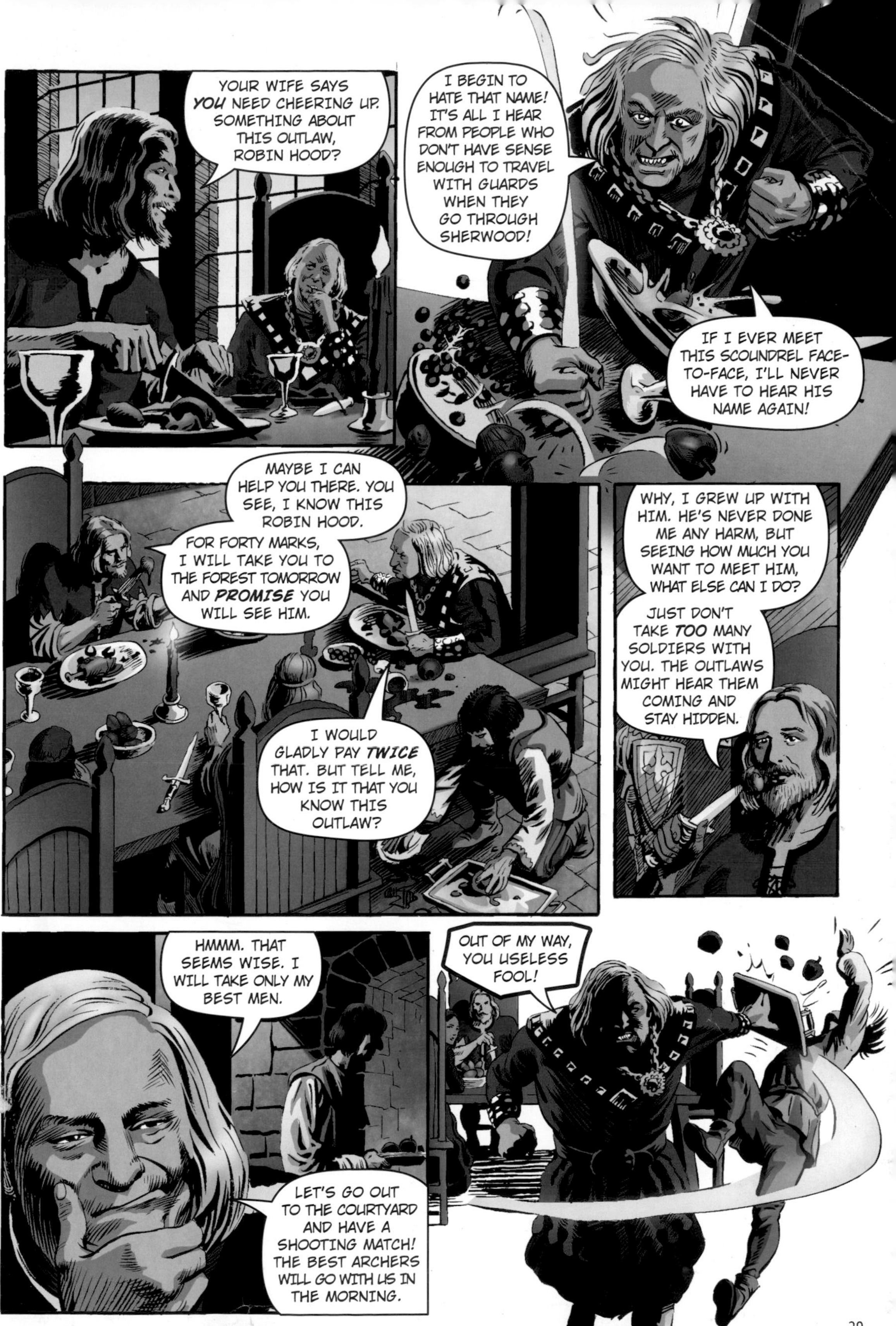

YOUR WIFE SAYS YOU NEED CHEERING UP. SOMETHING ABOUT THIS OUTLAW, ROBIN HOOD?
I BEGIN TO HATE THAT NAME! IT'S ALL I HEAR FROM PEOPLE WHO DON'T HAVE SENSE ENOUGH TO TRAVEL WITH GUARDS WHEN THEY GO THROUGH SHERWOOD!
IF I EVER MEET THIS SCOUNDREL FACE-TO-FACE, I'LL NEVER HAVE TO HEAR HIS NAME AGAIN!
MAYBE I CAN HELP YOU THERE. YOU SEE, I KNOW THIS ROBIN HOOD.
FOR FORTY MARKS, I WILL TAKE YOU TO THE FOREST TOMORROW AND PROMISE YOU WILL SEE HIM.
I WOULD GLADLY PAY TWICE THAT. BUT TELL ME, HOW IS IT THAT YOU KNOW THIS OUTLAW?
WHY, I GREW UP WITH HIM. HE'S NEVER DONE ME ANY HARM, BUT SEEING HOW MUCH YOU WANT TO MEET HIM, WHAT ELSE CAN I DO?
JUST DON'T TAKE TOO MANY SOLDIERS WITH YOU. THE OUTLAWS MIGHT HEAR THEM COMING AND STAY HIDDEN.
HMMM. THAT SEEMS WISE. I WILL TAKE ONLY MY BEST MEN.
LET'S GO OUT TO THE COURTYARD AND HAVE A SHOOTING MATCH! THE BEST ARCHERS WILL GO WITH US IN THE MORNING.
OUT OF MY WAY, YOU USELESS FOOL!

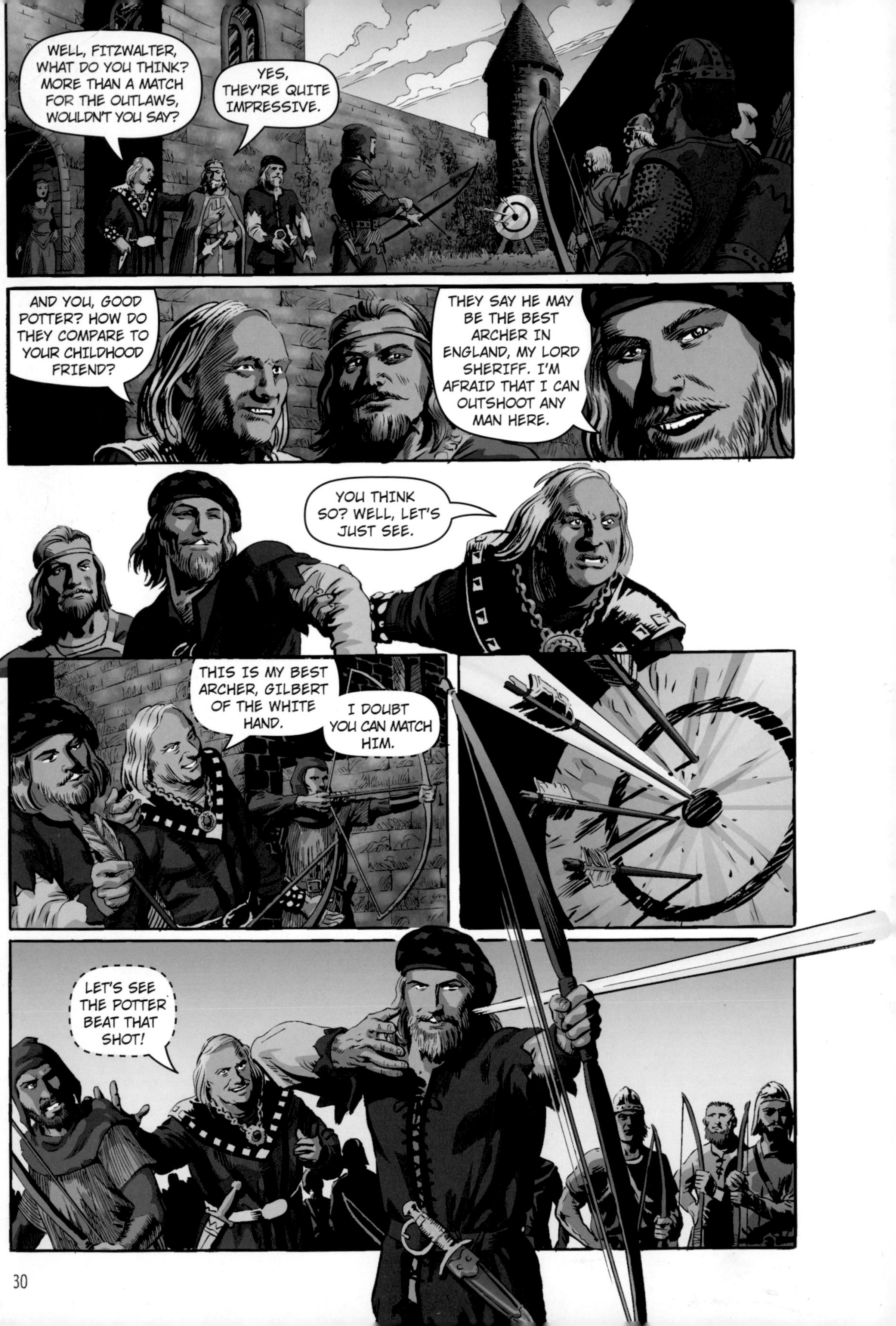

WELL, FITZWALTER, WHAT DO YOU THINK? MORE THAN A MATCH FOR THE OUTLAWS, WOULDN'T YOU SAY?
YES, THEY'RE QUITE IMPRESSIVE.
AND YOU, GOOD POTTER? HOW DO THEY COMPARE TO YOUR CHILDHOOD FRIEND?
THEY SAY HE MAY BE THE BEST ARCHER IN ENGLAND, MY LORD SHERIFF. I'M AFRAID THAT I CAN OUTSHOOT ANY MAN HERE.
YOU THINK SO? WELL, LET'S JUST SEE.
THIS IS MY BEST ARCHER, GILBERT OF THE WHITE HAND.
I DOUBT YOU CAN MATCH HIM.
LET'S SEE THE POTTER BEAT THAT SHOT!

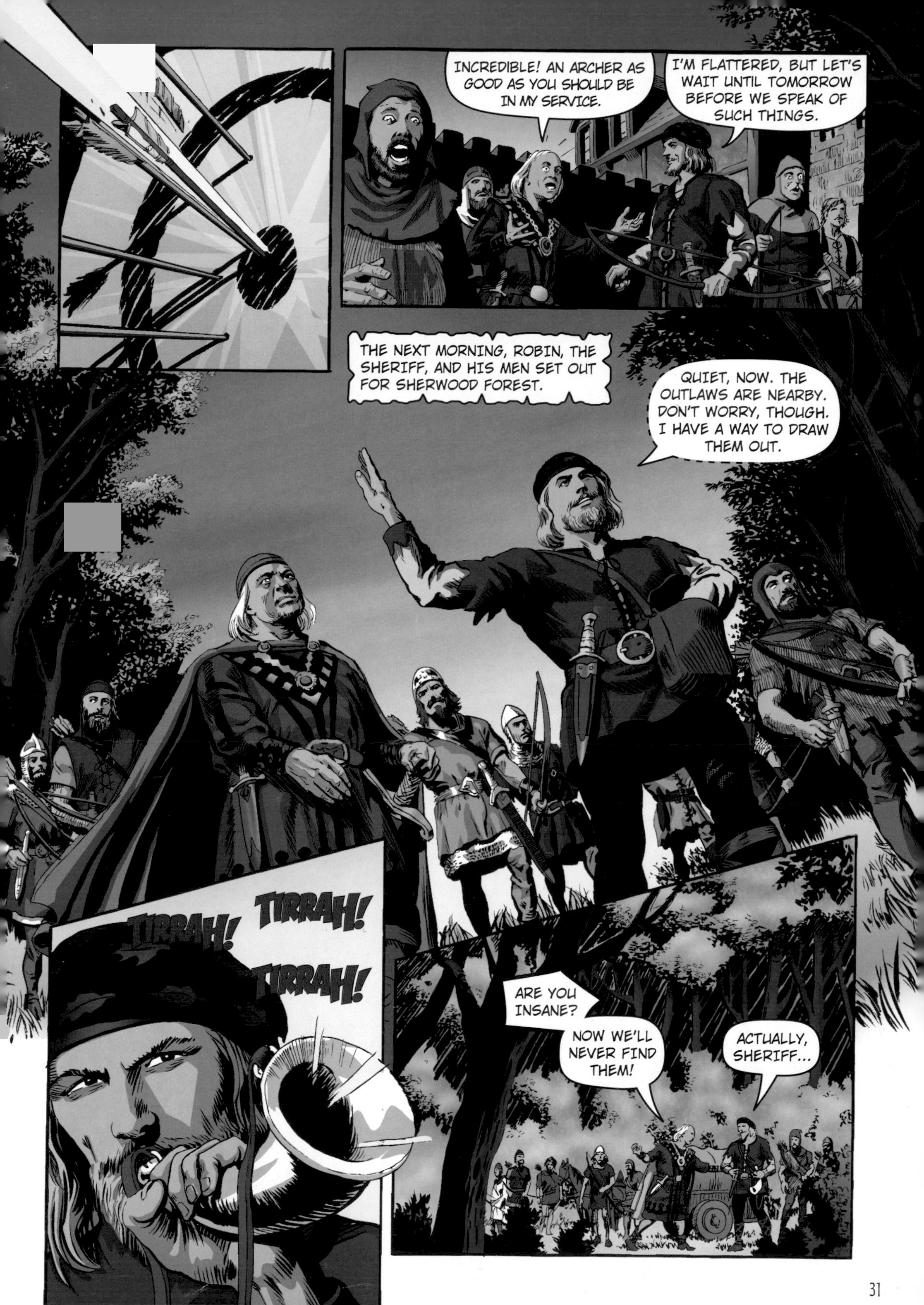
INCREDIBLE! AN ARCHER AS GOOD AS YOU SHOULD BE IN MY SERVICE.
I'M FLATTERED, BUT LET'S WAIT UNTIL TOMORROW BEFORE WE SPEAK OF SUCH THINGS.
THE NEXT MORNING, ROBIN, THE SHERIFF, AND HIS MEN SET OUT FOR SHERWOOD FOREST.
QUIET, NOW. THE OUTLAWS ARE NEARBY. DON'T WORRY, THOUGH. I HAVE A WAY TO DRAW THEM OUT.
TIRRAH!
TIRRAH!
TIRRAH!
ARE YOU INSANE?
NOW WE'LL NEVER FIND THEM!
ACTUALLY, SHERIFF...

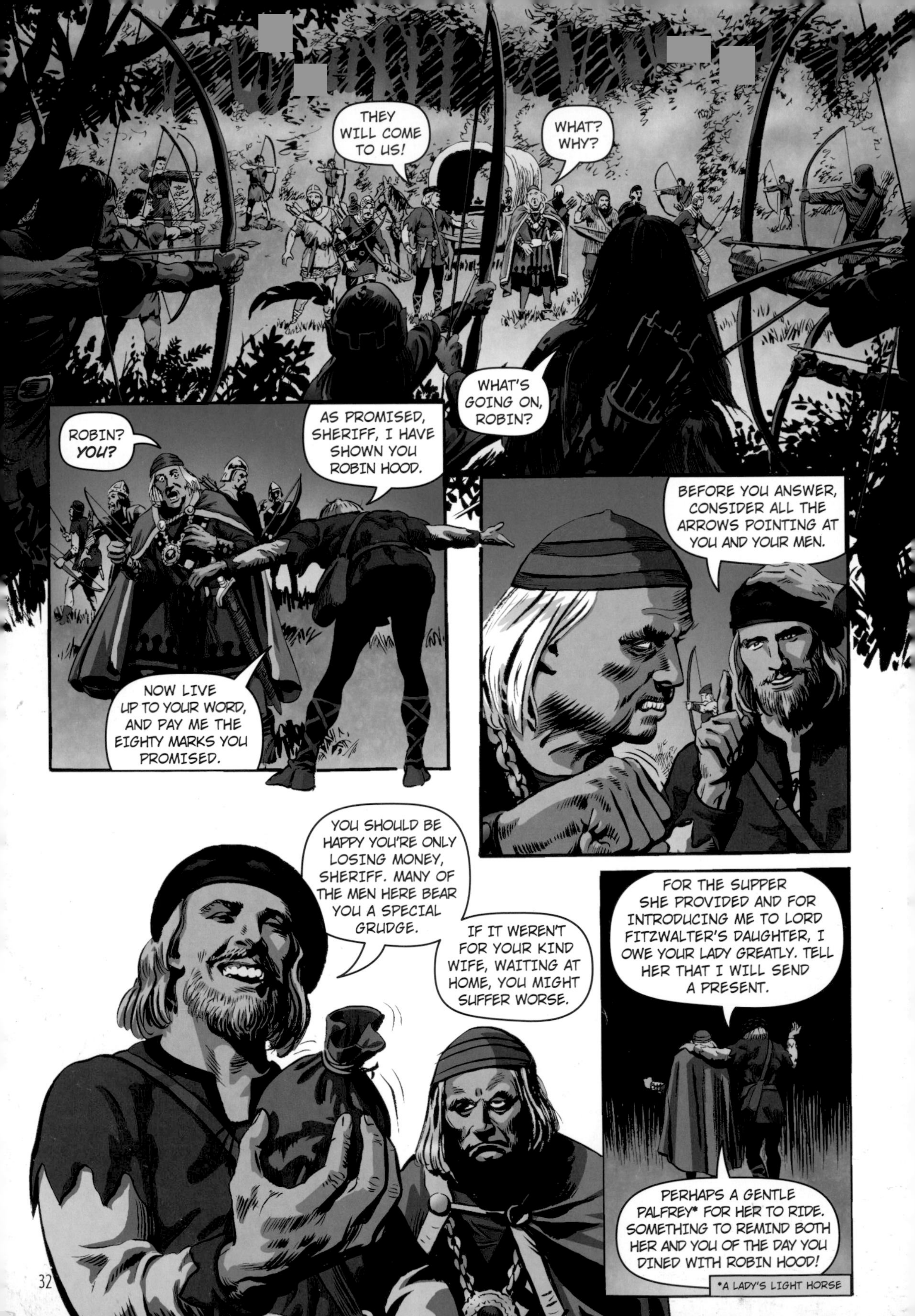
THEY WILL COME TO US!
WHAT? WHY?
WHAT'S GOING ON, ROBIN?
ROBIN? *YOU?*
AS PROMISED, SHERIFF, I HAVE SHOWN YOU ROBIN HOOD.
NOW LIVE UP TO YOUR WORD, AND PAY ME THE EIGHTY MARKS YOU PROMISED.
BEFORE YOU ANSWER, CONSIDER ALL THE ARROWS POINTING AT YOU AND YOUR MEN.
YOU SHOULD BE HAPPY YOU'RE ONLY LOSING MONEY, SHERIFF. MANY OF THE MEN HERE BEAR YOU A SPECIAL GRUDGE.
IF IT WEREN'T FOR YOUR KIND WIFE, WAITING AT HOME, YOU MIGHT SUFFER WORSE.
FOR THE SUPPER SHE PROVIDED AND FOR INTRODUCING ME TO LORD FITZWALTER'S DAUGHTER, I OWE YOUR LADY GREATLY. TELL HER THAT I WILL SEND A PRESENT.
PERHAPS A GENTLE PALFREY* FOR HER TO RIDE. SOMETHING TO REMIND BOTH HER AND YOU OF THE DAY YOU DINED WITH ROBIN HOOD!
*A LADY'S LIGHT HORSE

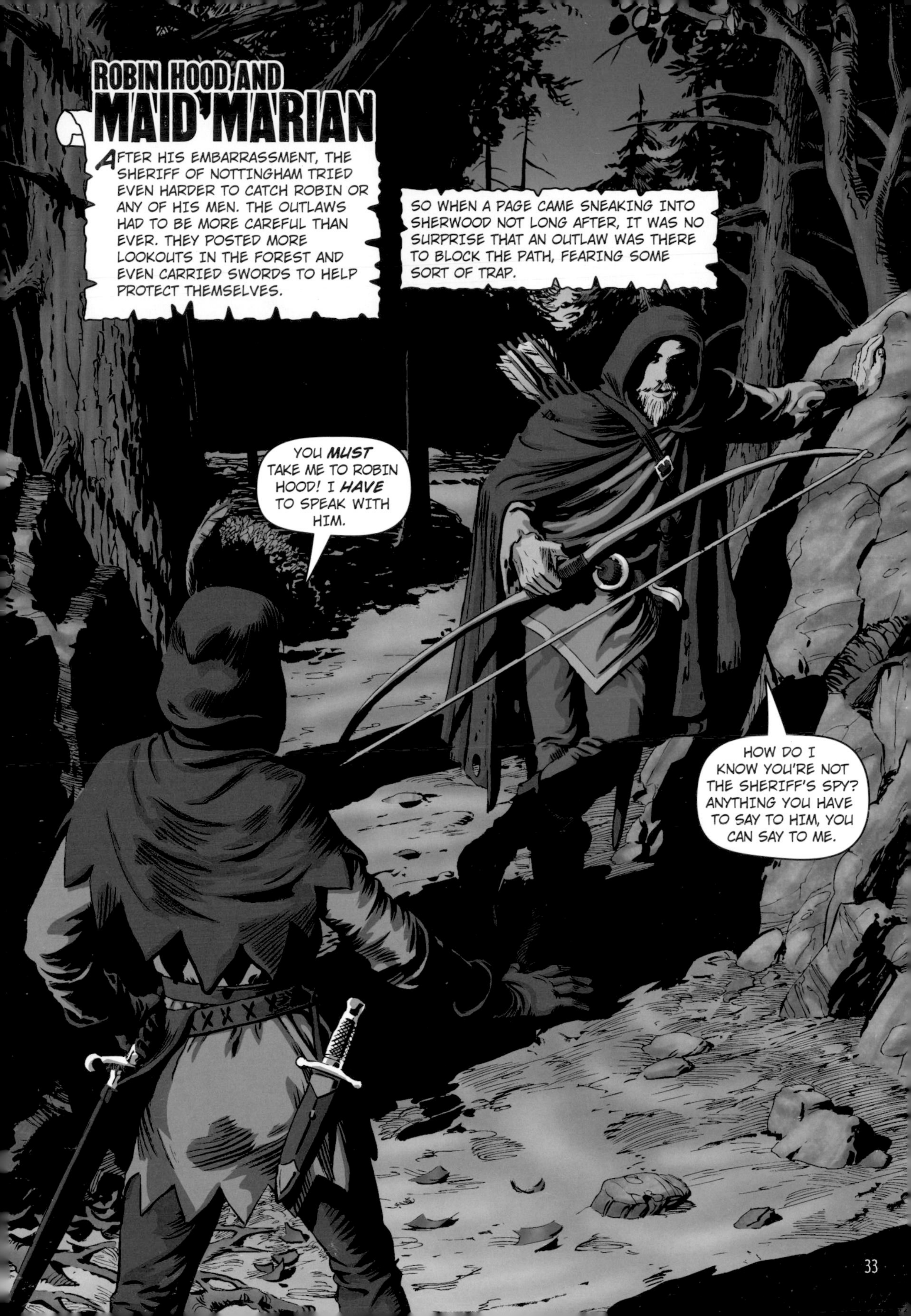

ROBIN HOOD AND MAID MARIAN
AFTER HIS EMBARRASSMENT, THE SHERIFF OF NOTTINGHAM TRIED EVEN HARDER TO CATCH ROBIN OR ANY OF HIS MEN. THE OUTLAWS HAD TO BE MORE CAREFUL THAN EVER. THEY POSTED MORE LOOKOUTS IN THE FOREST AND EVEN CARRIED SWORDS TO HELP PROTECT THEMSELVES.
SO WHEN A PAGE CAME SNEAKING INTO SHERWOOD NOT LONG AFTER, IT WAS NO SURPRISE THAT AN OUTLAW WAS THERE TO BLOCK THE PATH, FEARING SOME SORT OF TRAP.
YOU **MUST** TAKE ME TO ROBIN HOOD! I **HAVE** TO SPEAK WITH HIM.
HOW DO I KNOW YOU'RE NOT THE SHERIFF'S SPY? ANYTHING YOU HAVE TO SAY TO HIM, YOU CAN SAY TO ME.

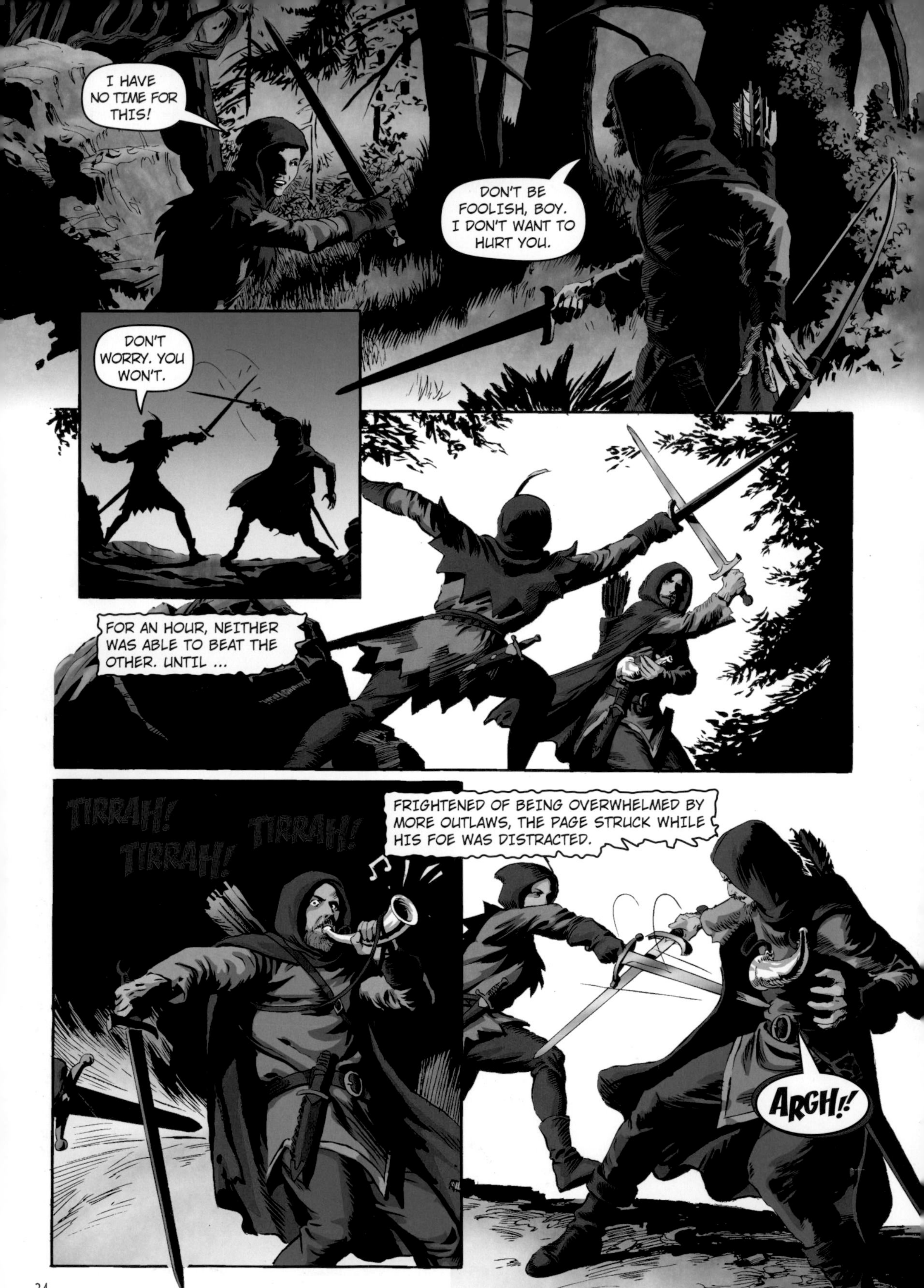
I HAVE NO TIME FOR THIS!
DON'T BE FOOLISH, BOY. I DON'T WANT TO HURT YOU.
DON'T WORRY. YOU WON'T.
FOR AN HOUR, NEITHER WAS ABLE TO BEAT THE OTHER. UNTIL ...
TIRRAH! TIRRAH! TIRRAH!
FRIGHTENED OF BEING OVERWHELMED BY MORE OUTLAWS, THE PAGE STRUCK WHILE HIS FOE WAS DISTRACTED.
ARGH!!

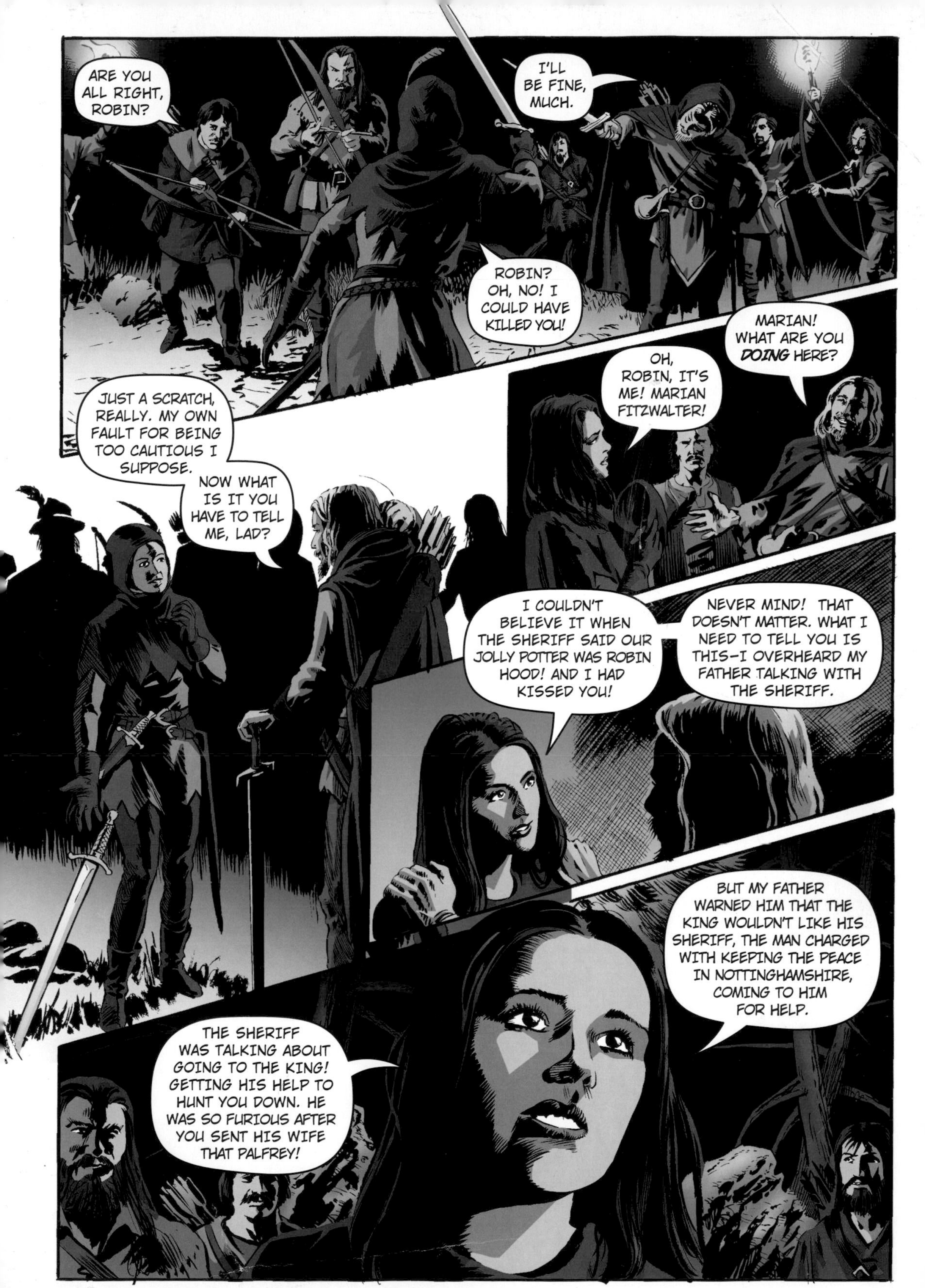
ARE YOU ALL RIGHT, ROBIN?
I'LL BE FINE, MUCH.
ROBIN? OH, NO! I COULD HAVE KILLED YOU!
OH, ROBIN, IT'S ME! MARIAN FITZWALTER!
MARIAN! WHAT ARE YOU DOING HERE?
JUST A SCRATCH, REALLY. MY OWN FAULT FOR BEING TOO CAUTIOUS I SUPPOSE.
NOW WHAT IS IT YOU HAVE TO TELL ME, LAD?
I COULDN'T BELIEVE IT WHEN THE SHERIFF SAID OUR JOLLY POTTER WAS ROBIN HOOD! AND I HAD KISSED YOU!
NEVER MIND! THAT DOESN'T MATTER. WHAT I NEED TO TELL YOU IS THIS—I OVERHEARD MY FATHER TALKING WITH THE SHERIFF.
THE SHERIFF WAS TALKING ABOUT GOING TO THE KING! GETTING HIS HELP TO HUNT YOU DOWN. HE WAS SO FURIOUS AFTER YOU SENT HIS WIFE THAT PALFREY!
BUT MY FATHER WARNED HIM THAT THE KING WOULDN'T LIKE HIS SHERIFF, THE MAN CHARGED WITH KEEPING THE PEACE IN NOTTINGHAMSHIRE, COMING TO HIM FOR HELP.

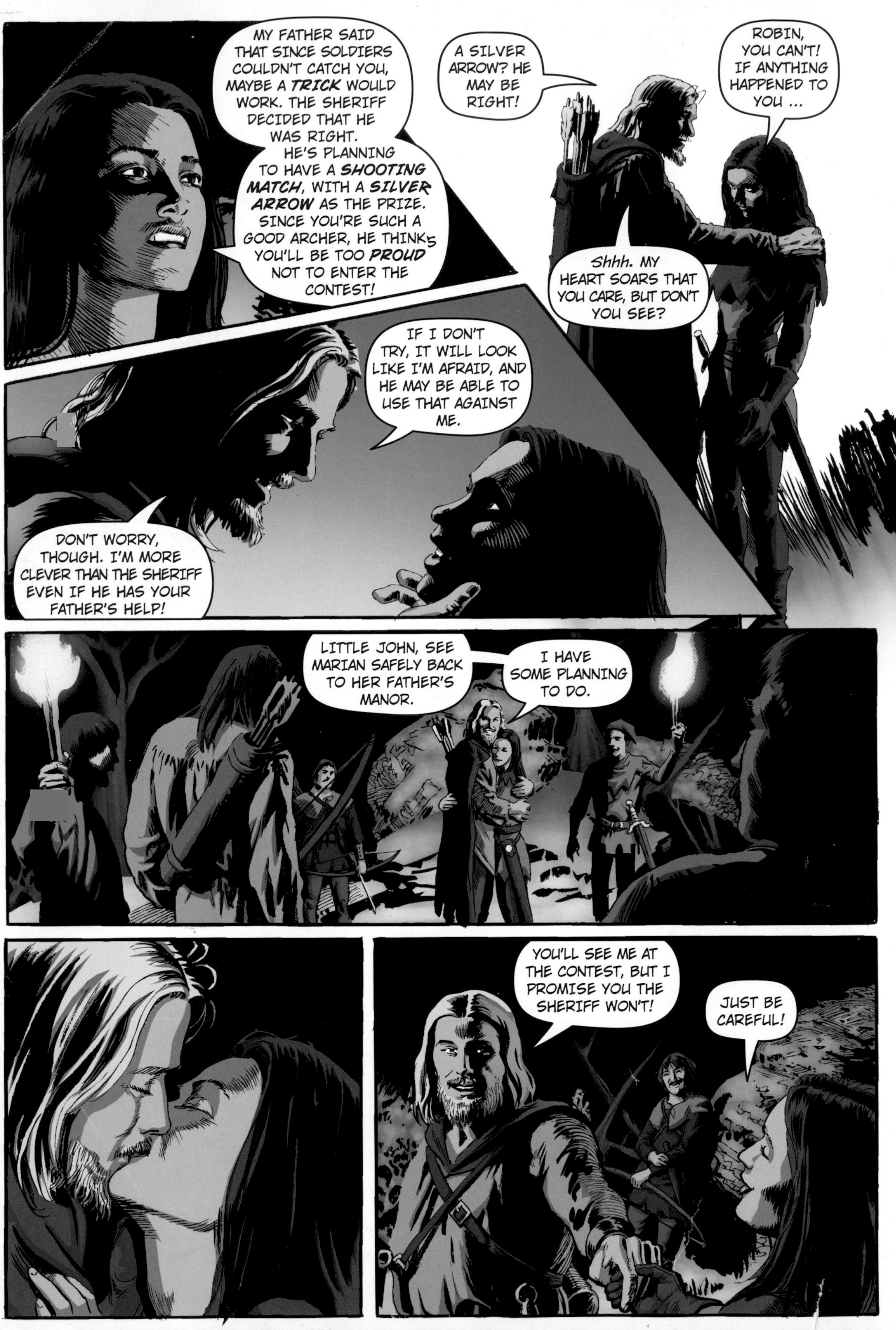
MY FATHER SAID THAT SINCE SOLDIERS COULDN'T CATCH YOU, MAYBE A TRICK WOULD WORK. THE SHERIFF DECIDED THAT HE WAS RIGHT.
HE'S PLANNING TO HAVE A SHOOTING MATCH, WITH A SILVER ARROW AS THE PRIZE. SINCE YOU'RE SUCH A GOOD ARCHER, HE THINKS YOU'LL BE TOO PROUD NOT TO ENTER THE CONTEST!
A SILVER ARROW? HE MAY BE RIGHT!
ROBIN, YOU CAN'T! IF ANYTHING HAPPENED TO YOU ...
Shhh. MY HEART SOARS THAT YOU CARE, BUT DON'T YOU SEE?
IF I DON'T TRY, IT WILL LOOK LIKE I'M AFRAID, AND HE MAY BE ABLE TO USE THAT AGAINST ME.
DON'T WORRY, THOUGH. I'M MORE CLEVER THAN THE SHERIFF EVEN IF HE HAS YOUR FATHER'S HELP!
LITTLE JOHN, SEE MARIAN SAFELY BACK TO HER FATHER'S MANOR.
I HAVE SOME PLANNING TO DO.
YOU'LL SEE ME AT THE CONTEST, BUT I PROMISE YOU THE SHERIFF WON'T!
JUST BE CAREFUL!

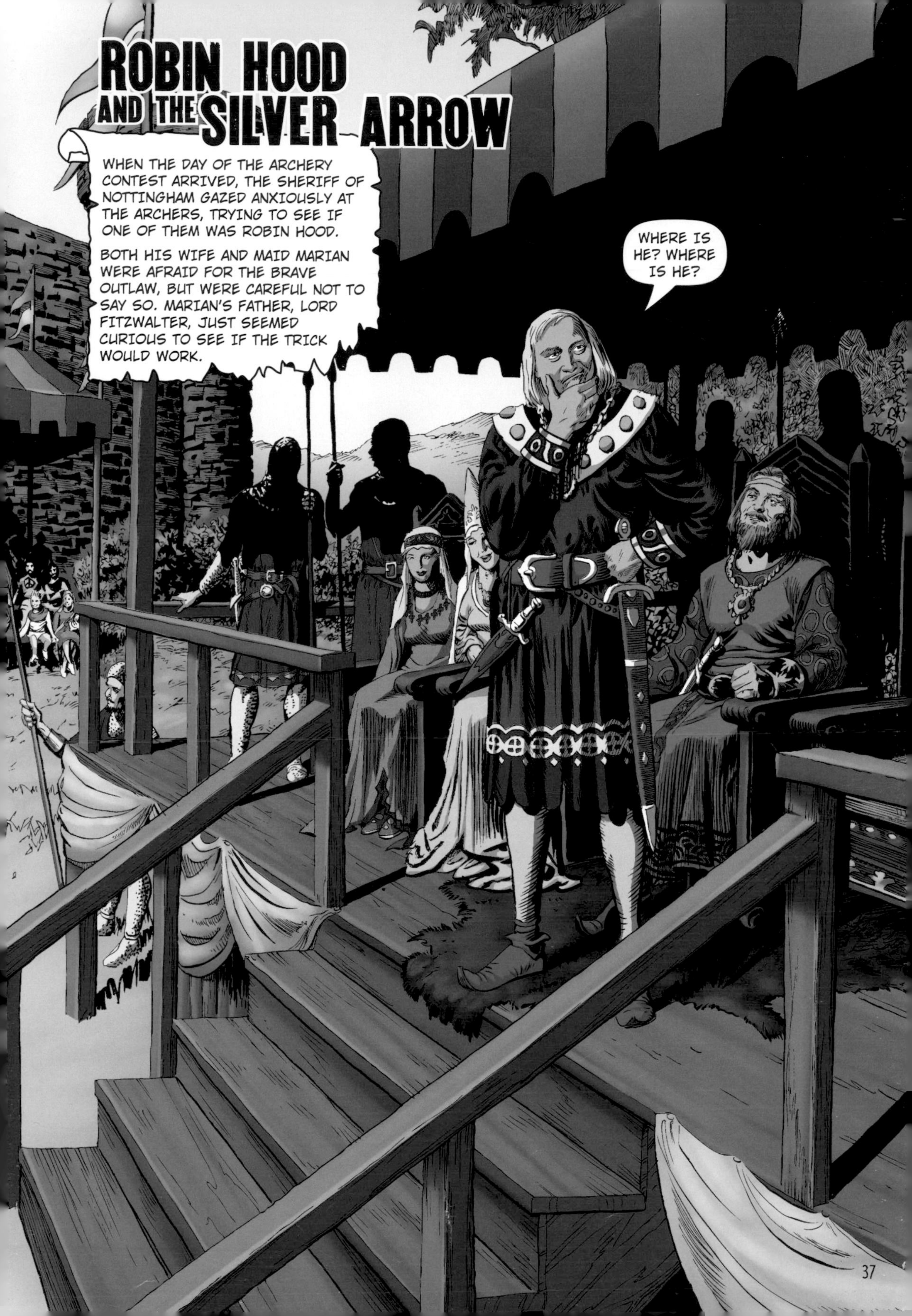
ROBIN HOOD AND THE SILVER ARROW
WHEN THE DAY OF THE ARCHERY CONTEST ARRIVED, THE SHERIFF OF NOTTINGHAM GAZED ANXIOUSLY AT THE ARCHERS, TRYING TO SEE IF ONE OF THEM WAS ROBIN HOOD.
BOTH HIS WIFE AND MAID MARIAN WERE AFRAID FOR THE BRAVE OUTLAW, BUT WERE CAREFUL NOT TO SAY SO. MARIAN'S FATHER, LORD FITZWALTER, JUST SEEMED CURIOUS TO SEE IF THE TRICK WOULD WORK.
WHERE IS HE? WHERE IS HE?

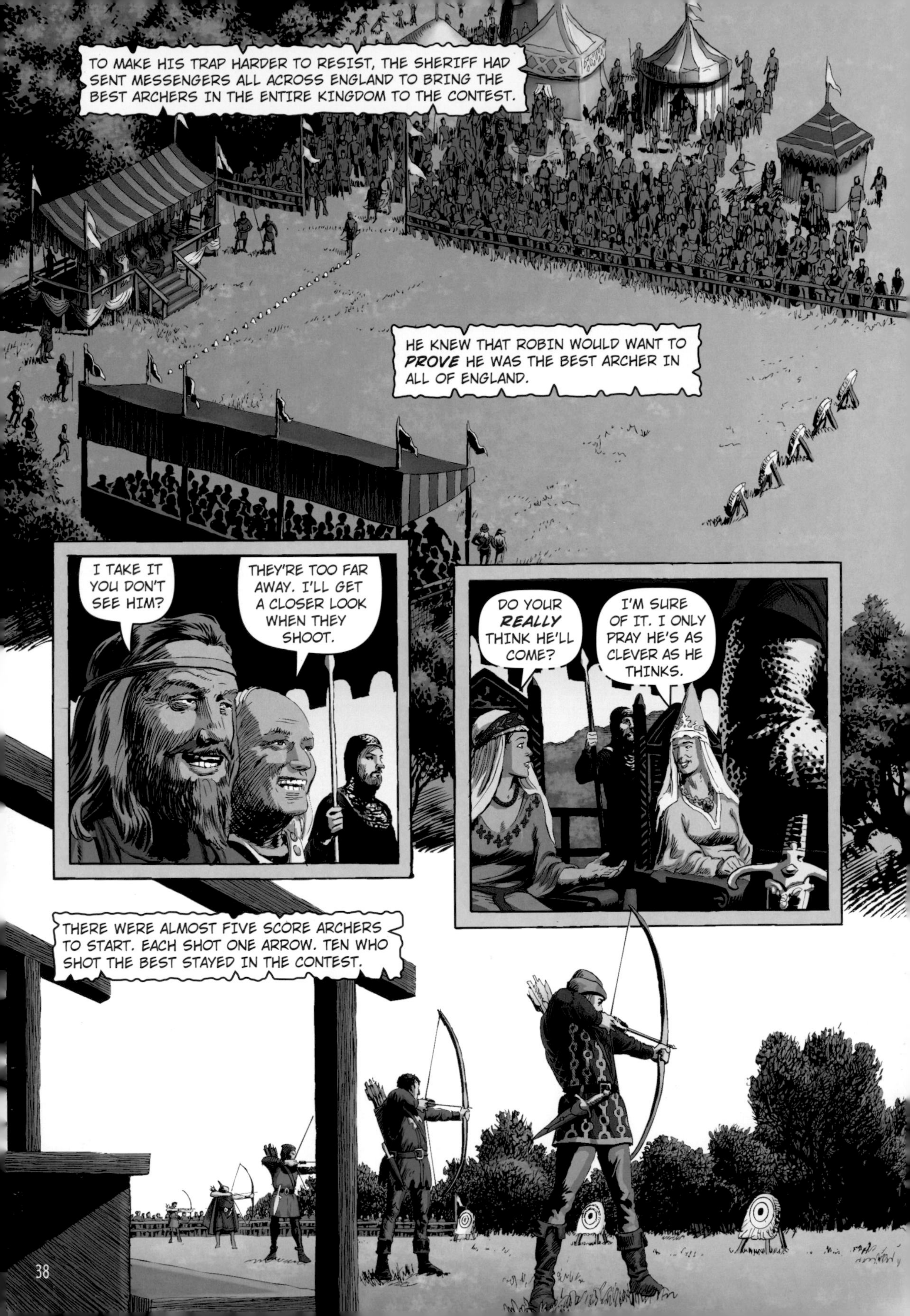
TO MAKE HIS TRAP HARDER TO RESIST, THE SHERIFF HAD SENT MESSENGERS ALL ACROSS ENGLAND TO BRING THE BEST ARCHERS IN THE ENTIRE KINGDOM TO THE CONTEST.
HE KNEW THAT ROBIN WOULD WANT TO *PROVE* HE WAS THE BEST ARCHER IN ALL OF ENGLAND.
I TAKE IT YOU DON'T SEE HIM?
THEY'RE TOO FAR AWAY. I'LL GET A CLOSER LOOK WHEN THEY SHOOT.
DO YOUR *REALLY* THINK HE'LL COME?
I'M SURE OF IT. I ONLY PRAY HE'S AS CLEVER AS HE THINKS.
THERE WERE ALMOST FIVE SCORE ARCHERS TO START. EACH SHOT ONE ARROW. TEN WHO SHOT THE BEST STAYED IN THE CONTEST.

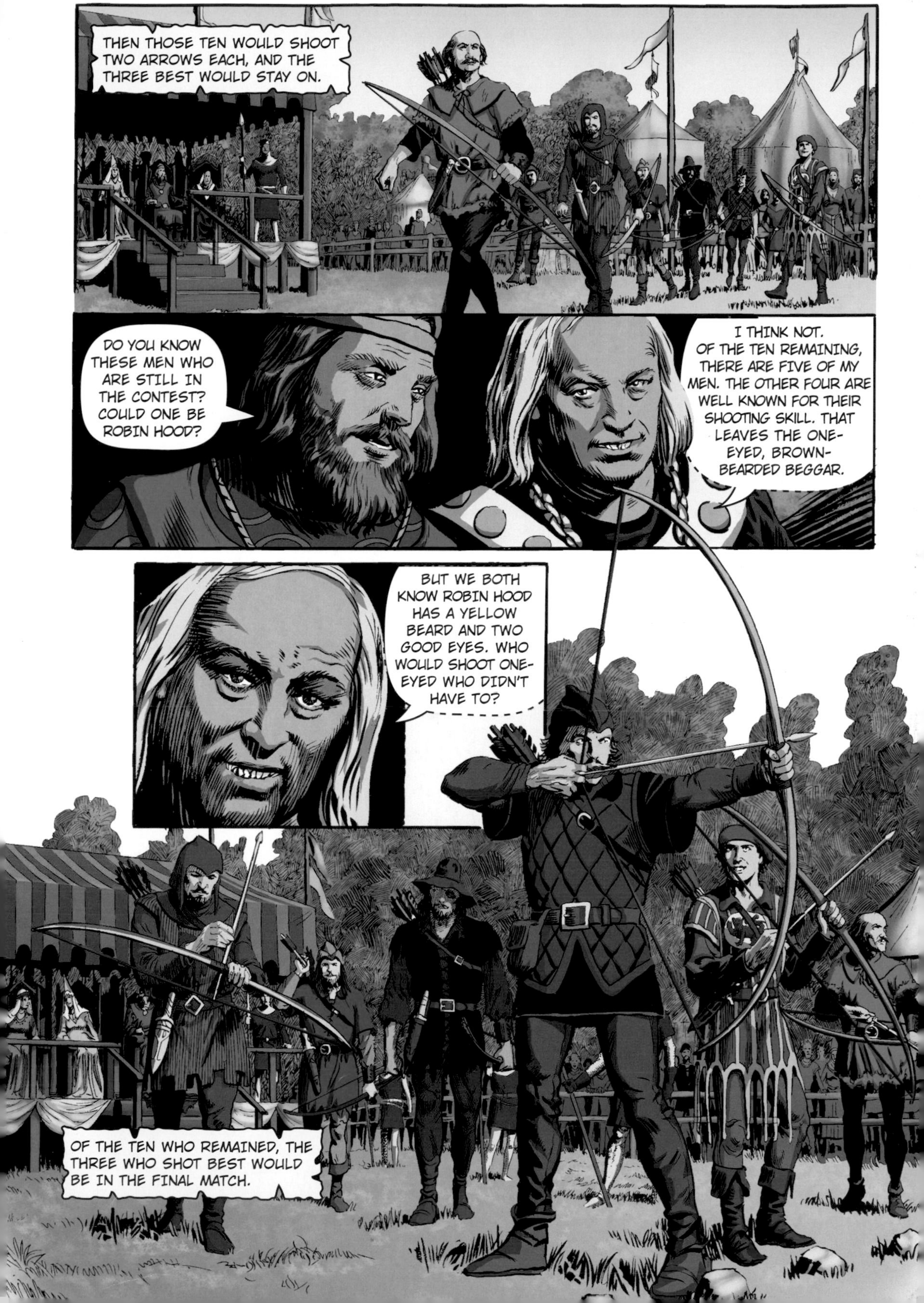
THEN THOSE TEN WOULD SHOOT TWO ARROWS EACH, AND THE THREE BEST WOULD STAY ON.
DO YOU KNOW THESE MEN WHO ARE STILL IN THE CONTEST? COULD ONE BE ROBIN HOOD?
I THINK NOT. OF THE TEN REMAINING, THERE ARE FIVE OF MY MEN. THE OTHER FOUR ARE WELL KNOWN FOR THEIR SHOOTING SKILL. THAT LEAVES THE ONE-EYED, BROWN-BEARDED BEGGAR.
BUT WE BOTH KNOW ROBIN HOOD HAS A YELLOW BEARD AND TWO GOOD EYES. WHO WOULD SHOOT ONE-EYED WHO DIDN'T HAVE TO?
OF THE TEN WHO REMAINED, THE THREE WHO SHOT BEST WOULD BE IN THE FINAL MATCH.

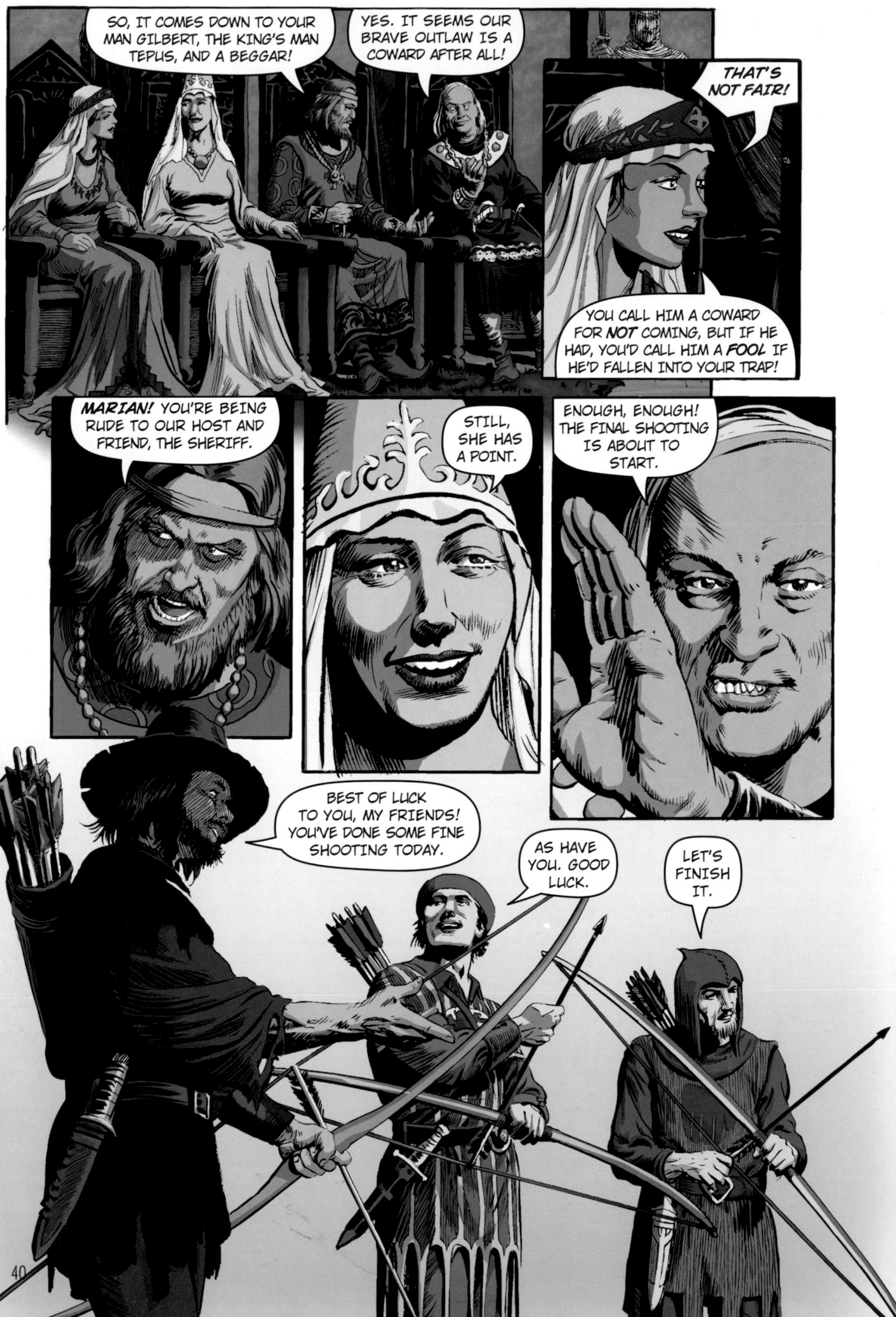
SO, IT COMES DOWN TO YOUR MAN GILBERT, THE KING'S MAN TEPUS, AND A BEGGAR!
YES. IT SEEMS OUR BRAVE OUTLAW IS A COWARD AFTER ALL!
THAT'S NOT FAIR!
YOU CALL HIM A COWARD FOR NOT COMING, BUT IF HE HAD, YOU'D CALL HIM A FOOL IF HE'D FALLEN INTO YOUR TRAP!
MARIAN! YOU'RE BEING RUDE TO OUR HOST AND FRIEND, THE SHERIFF.
STILL, SHE HAS A POINT.
ENOUGH, ENOUGH! THE FINAL SHOOTING IS ABOUT TO START.
BEST OF LUCK TO YOU, MY FRIENDS! YOU'VE DONE SOME FINE SHOOTING TODAY.
AS HAVE YOU. GOOD LUCK.
LET'S FINISH IT.

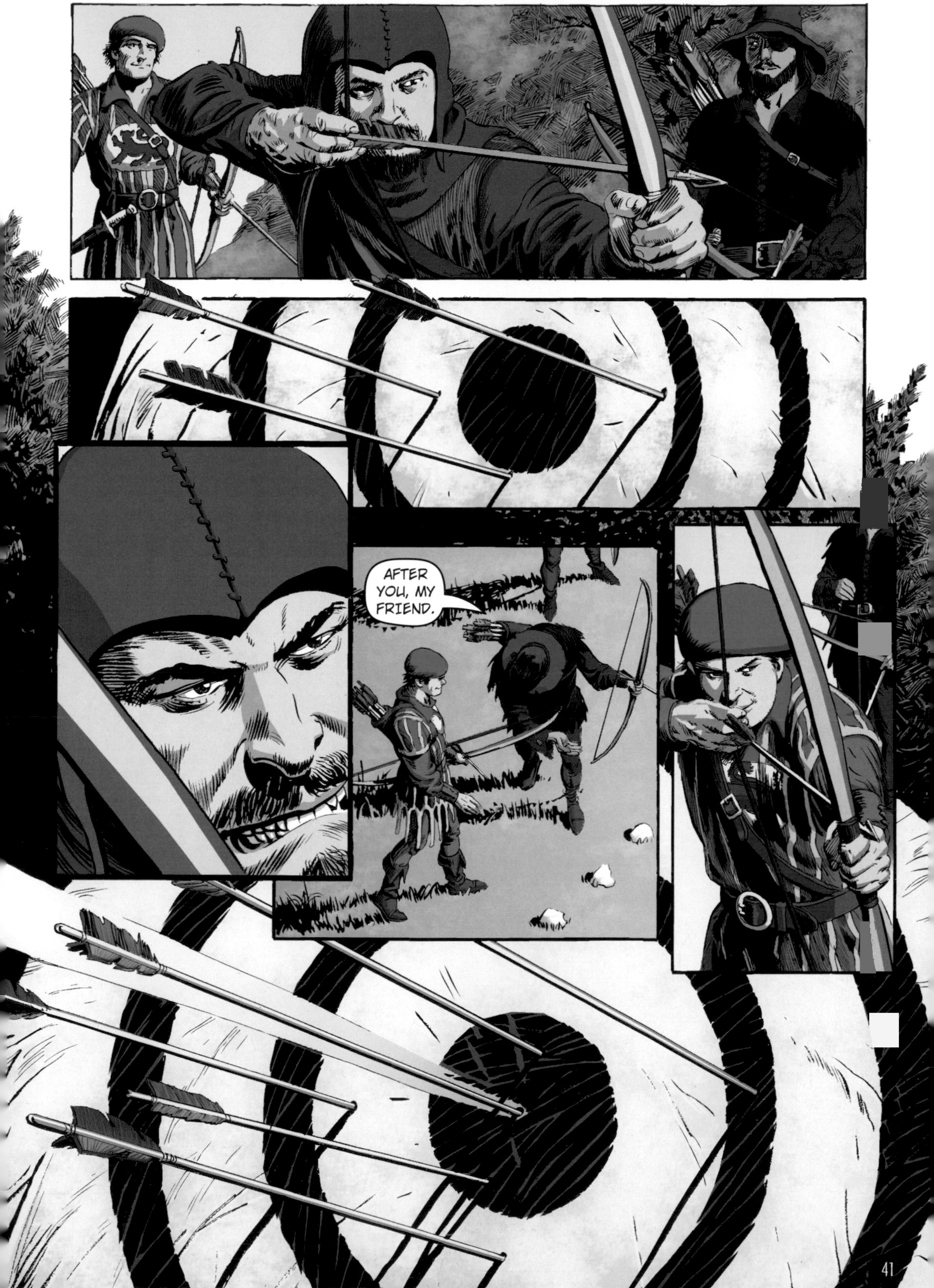
AFTER YOU, MY FRIEND.

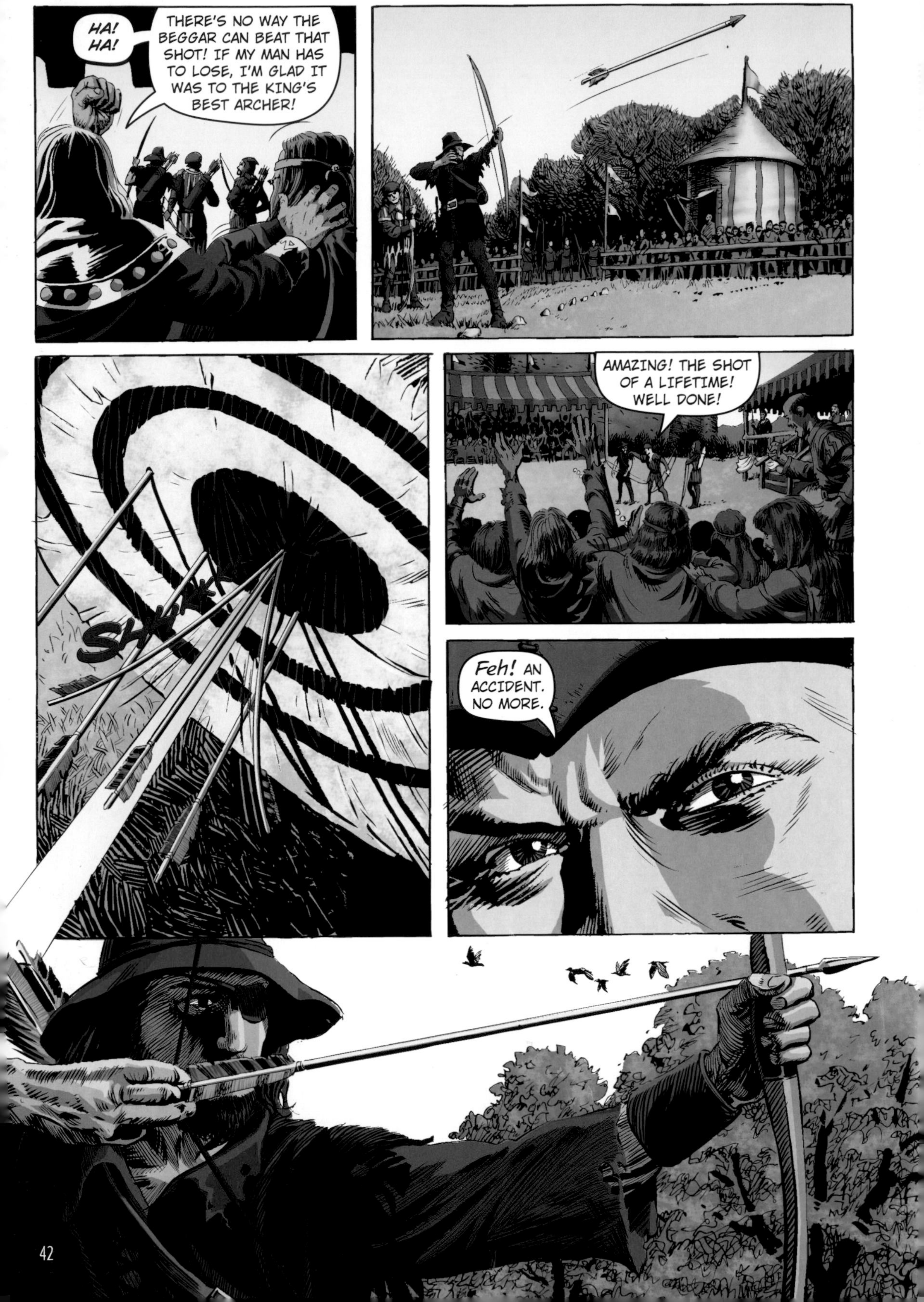
HA! HA!
THERE'S NO WAY THE BEGGAR CAN BEAT THAT SHOT! IF MY MAN HAS TO LOSE, I'M GLAD IT WAS TO THE KING'S BEST ARCHER!
SHUKK
AMAZING! THE SHOT OF A LIFETIME! WELL DONE!
Feh! AN ACCIDENT. NO MORE.

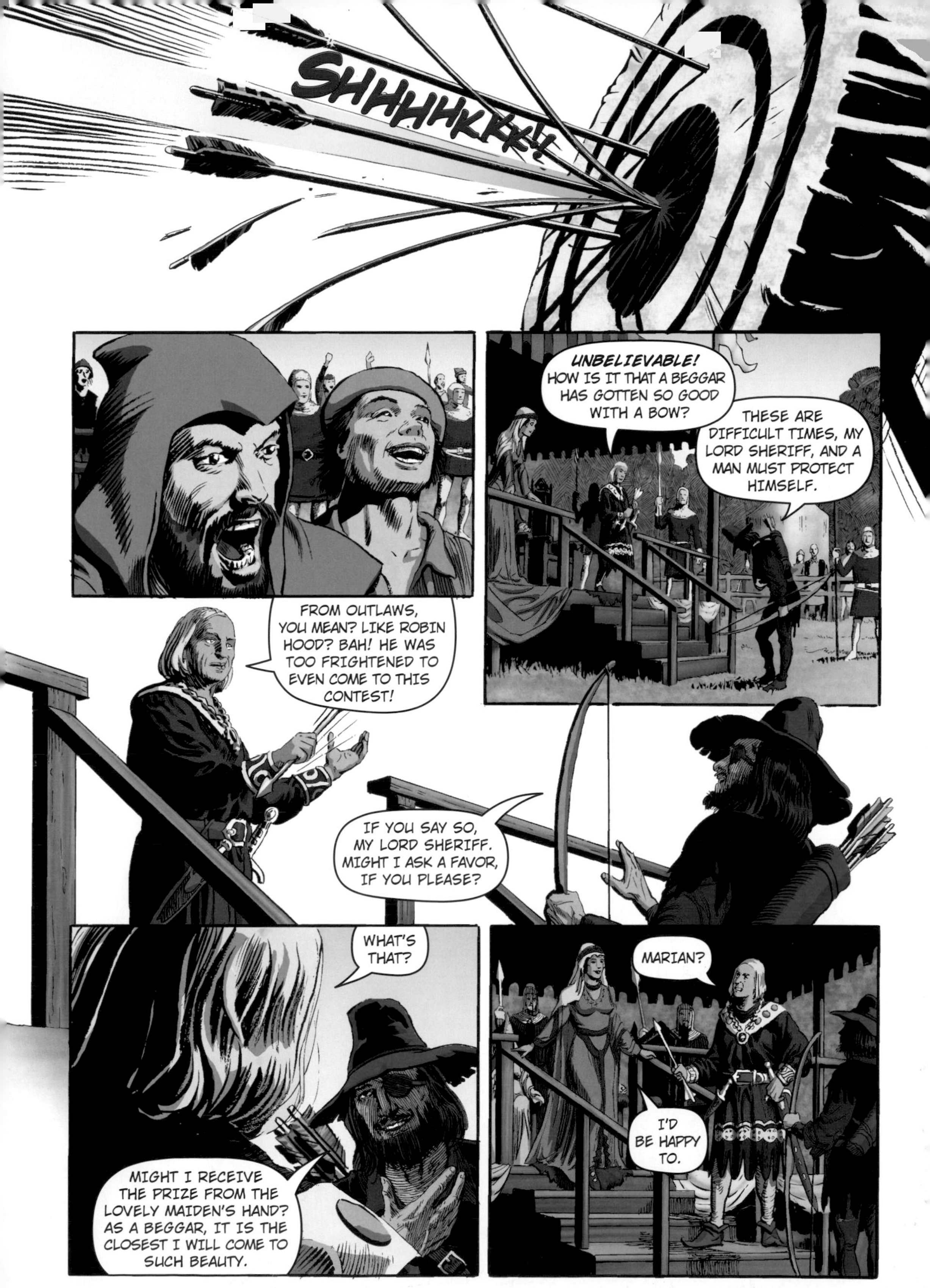

SHHHHKKK!!
UNBELIEVABLE! HOW IS IT THAT A BEGGAR HAS GOTTEN SO GOOD WITH A BOW?
THESE ARE DIFFICULT TIMES, MY LORD SHERIFF, AND A MAN MUST PROTECT HIMSELF.
FROM OUTLAWS, YOU MEAN? LIKE ROBIN HOOD? BAH! HE WAS TOO FRIGHTENED TO EVEN COME TO THIS CONTEST!
IF YOU SAY SO, MY LORD SHERIFF. MIGHT I ASK A FAVOR, IF YOU PLEASE?
WHAT'S THAT?
MIGHT I RECEIVE THE PRIZE FROM THE LOVELY MAIDEN'S HAND? AS A BEGGAR, IT IS THE CLOSEST I WILL COME TO SUCH BEAUTY.
MARIAN?
I'D BE HAPPY TO.

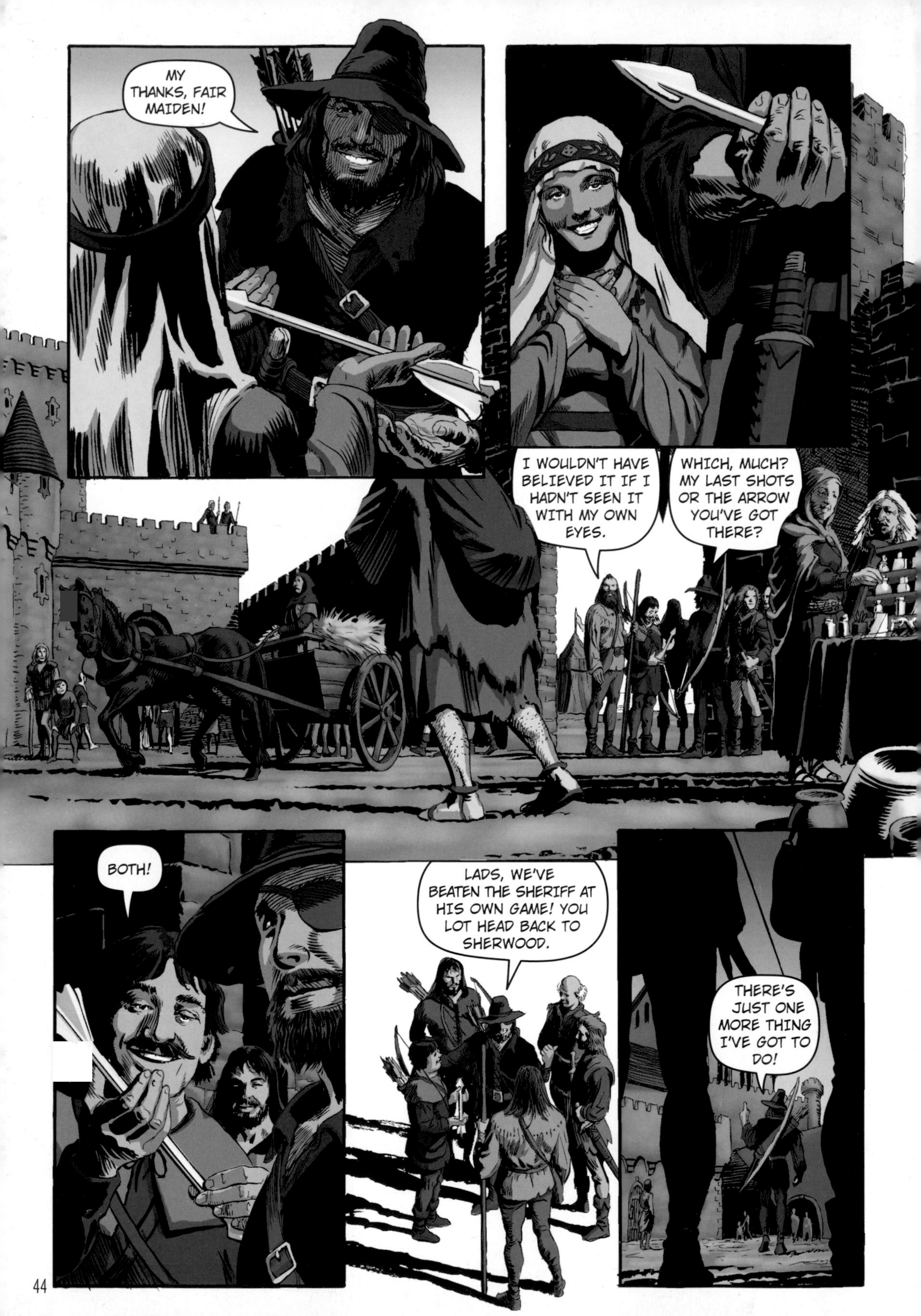
MY THANKS, FAIR MAIDEN!
I WOULDN'T HAVE BELIEVED IT IF I HADN'T SEEN IT WITH MY OWN EYES.
WHICH, MUCH? MY LAST SHOTS OR THE ARROW YOU'VE GOT THERE?
BOTH!
LADS, WE'VE BEATEN THE SHERIFF AT HIS OWN GAME! YOU LOT HEAD BACK TO SHERWOOD.
THERE'S JUST ONE MORE THING I'VE GOT TO DO!

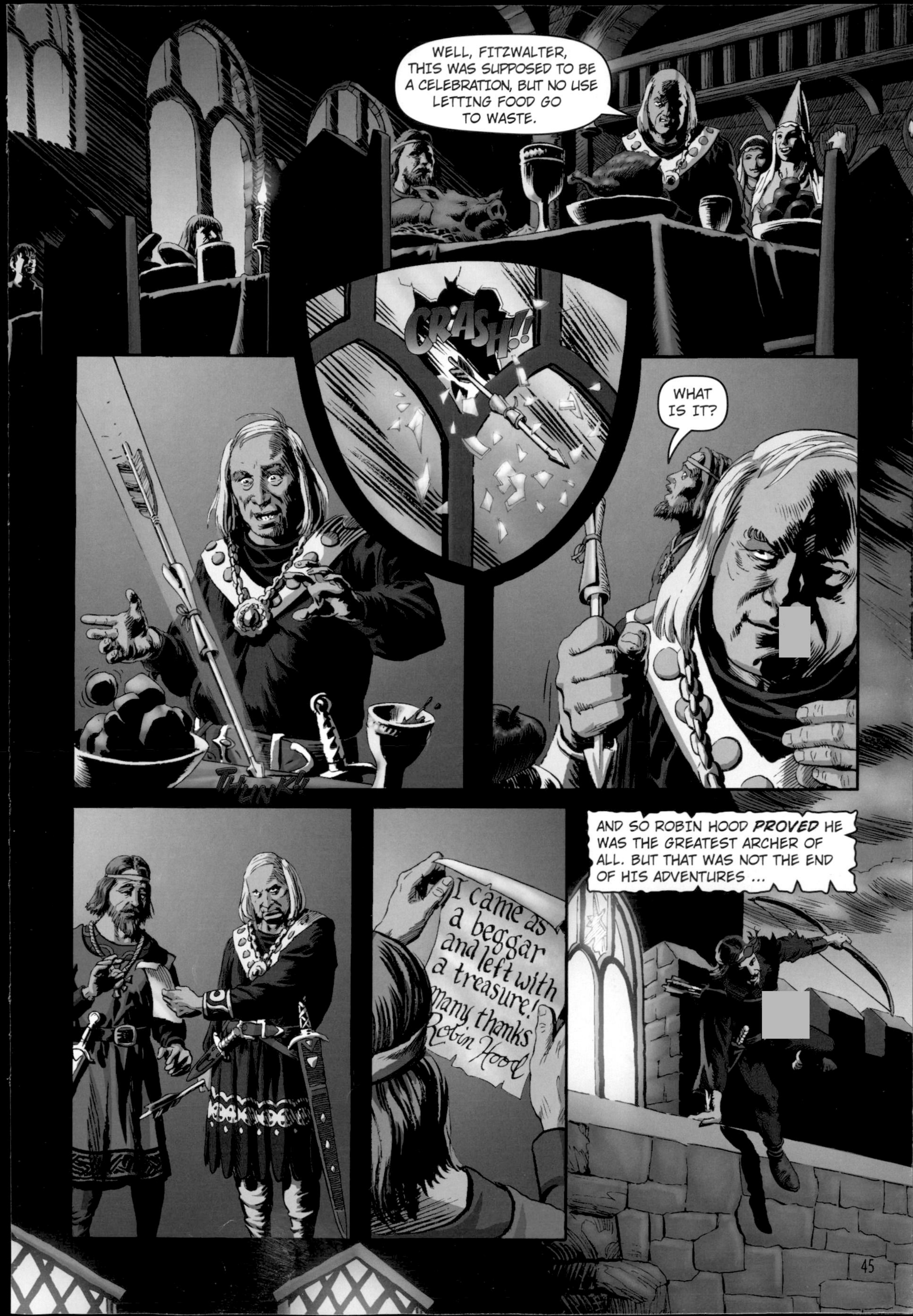
WELL, FITZWALTER, THIS WAS SUPPOSED TO BE A CELEBRATION, BUT NO USE LETTING FOOD GO TO WASTE.
CRASH!!
THUNK!!
WHAT IS IT?
AND SO ROBIN HOOD **PROVED** HE WAS THE GREATEST ARCHER OF ALL. BUT THAT WAS NOT THE END OF HIS ADVENTURES ...
I came as a beggar and left with a treasure! many thanks Robin Hood

GLOSSARY AND PRONUNCIATION GUIDE

ARCHER: a person who uses a bow and arrow

BEGGAR: a person who lives by asking for food or money

BOON: a timely benefit; a blessing

FORESTER: a man hired to guard the forest from outlaws

KNIGHT: a man devoted to the service of a superior, such as a king or lord

LORD: an English nobleman

MAIDEN: an unmarried girl or woman

MARK: an old English unit of currency

MILLER: a person who grinds grain into flour

NOBLEMAN: a man of high rank; an aristocrat

PALFREY (*pahl*-free): a lady's light horse

POTTER: a person who makes pottery

QUARTERSTAFF: a long staff used for fighting

SCORE: twenty things

SCOUNDREL: a rascal, troublemaker

TRADESMAN: a worker in a skilled trade

YEOMAN (*yoh*-mun): a middle-class English landowner

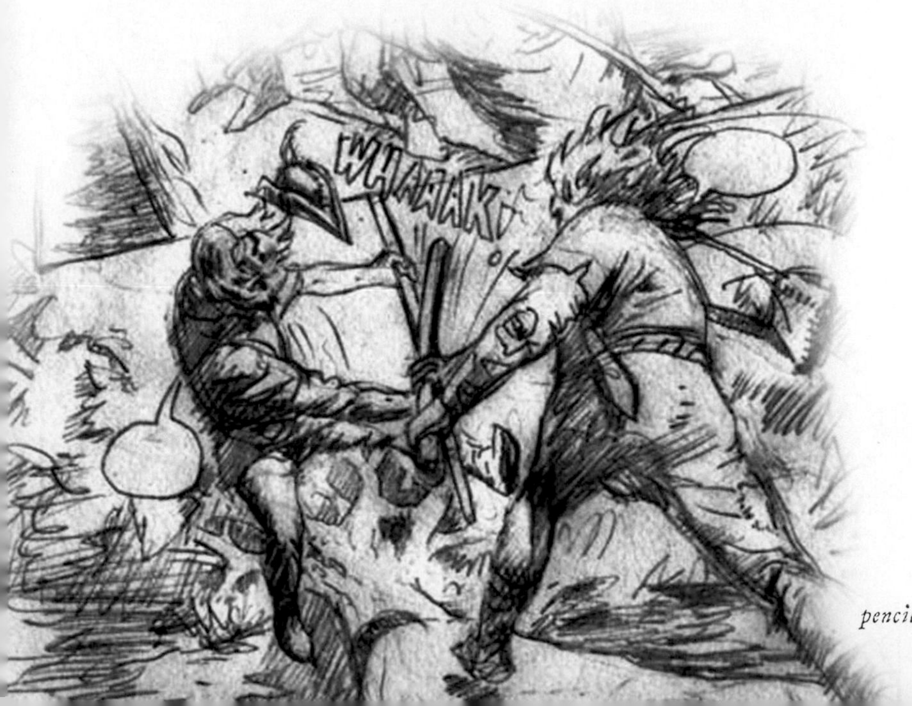
WHAAAK

pencil sketch from page 18

FURTHER READING, WEBSITES, AND MOVIES

The Adventures of Robin Hood. DVD. Directed by Michael Curtiz. Hollywood: Warner Bros. Pictures, 1938. This fun and exciting film, starring Errol Flynn as Robin and Olivia De Havilland as Maid Marian, is one of the most popular movies of all time.

Edens, Cooper. *Robin Hood: A Classic Illustrated Edition.* San Francisco: Chronicle Books, 2002. This book features tales of Robin Hood with illustrations dating from the twelfth to the twentieth centuries.

The Geste of Robin Hood
http://web.ics.purdue.edu/~ohlgren/gesttrans.html
Visit this website to read a contemporary translation of one of the original ballads of Robin Hood's adventures. The original geste (folk song) was composed in Middle English in the fifteenth century.

Pyle, Howard. *The Merry Adventures of Robin Hood.* New York: Signet Classics, 1986. Howard Pyle's illustrated adaptations of the Robin Hood stories are some of the most famous and popular in the world.

Robin Hood. DVD. Directed by John Irvin. Hollywood: 20th Century Fox, 1991. This action-packed made-for-TV movie stars Patrick Bergin as Robin and Uma Thurman as Maid Marian.

Robin Hood: A Beginner's Guide to Robin Hood
http://www.boldoutlaw.com/robbeg/robbeg1.html
This Web page provides a brief overview of the legend of Robin Hood and his many adventures. The page is part of a larger site that features a great deal of helpful information about the Outlaw of Sherwood.

CREATING *ROBIN HOOD: OUTLAW OF SHERWOOD FOREST*

Author Paul D. Storrie relied heavily on the earliest versions of the Robin Hood stories available: the lyrics to the medieval songs about Robin and his followers. His research also included the excellent books *Robin Hood* by J. C. Holt and *Robin Hood: A Complete Study of the English Outlaw* by Stephen Thomas Knight. Artist Thomas Yeates referred to modern sources of medieval dress as well as to illustrations by great artists of the past, including Howard Pyle, Harold Foster, and N. C. Wyeth. Professor Andrew Scheil of the University of Minnesota lent his time and expertise in reviewing this project.

INDEX

ABOUT THE AUTHOR AND THE ARTIST

PAUL D. STORRIE was born and raised in Detroit, Michigan, and has returned to live there again and again after living in other cities and states. He has been a fan of Robin Hood tales his entire life, and his very first published work was the 1987 comic book series Robyn of Sherwood about the daughter of the legendary archer. Since then, he has written several comic book stories about Robin Hood himself. His other works includes *Batman Beyond, Justice League Adventures,* and *Gotham Girls* for DC Comics and contributions to *Captain America: Red, White & Blue* and *Mutant X: Dangerous Decisions* for Marvel. He has also written *Hercules: The Twelve Labors* in the Graphic Myths and Legends series.

THOMAS YEATES Originally from Sacramento, California, Thomas Yeates began his art training in high school and continued it at Utah State University and at Sacramento State. Subsequently, he was a member of the first class at Joe Kubert's School, a trade program for aspiring comic book artists in New Jersey. Yeates is strongly influenced in his craft by old-guard illustrators like Hal Foster, N. C. Wyeth, and Wallace Wood. He has worked as an illustrator for DC, Marvel, Dark Horse, and many other companies, drawing *Tarzan, Zorro, the Swamp Thing, Timespirits, Captain America,* and *Conan,* among others. He has also edited *Al Williamson: Hidden Lands* for Dark Horse.